The perfect fit in men's tailoring

Adjust your patterns easily

The perfect fit in men's tailoring

Adjust your patterns easily

Sven Jungclaus

Bibliografische Information der Deutschen Nationalbibliothek:
Die Deutsche Nationalbibliothek verzeichnet diese Publikation
in der Deutschen Nationalbibliografie; detaillierte bibliografische
Daten sind im Internet über www.dnb.de abrufbar.

© 2021 Sven Jungclaus
1st correction

Herstellung und Verlag:
BoD – Books on Demand, Norderstedt
ISBN 9783751984416

Contents

8 Preface
9 Taking measurements
14 Taken measurements in a pattern
19 Body shape and posture
23 Perfect fit and how to do a fitting

The pants
34 Pelvis tilted forward
35 Pelvis tilted backward
36 Raising the waistline at the side seam
37 Lowering the waistline at the side seam
38 Pelvis tilted sideways
39 Hip is stronger on one side
40 Knock-knees
41 Bowlegs
42 Extending the waistband
43 Reducing the waistband
44 Strong hip curve
45 Flat hip curve
46 Flat seat
47 Strong seat
48 Extending the crotch
49 Reducing the crotch
50 Room at the back of the pants
51 Lowering the rise
51 Lifting the rise
52 Considering the "package"
53 Pleat opens up
53 Too tight at the calf
54 Extending the thigh girth
55 Reducing the thigh girth
56 Extending the hem girth
57 Reducing the hem girth

Tailoring the pants
58 Pressing pants properly

The vest
60 Stooped posture
61 Rounded back
62 S-shape posture
63 Erect posture

The vest
64 Vest is too tight
65 Vest is too loose
66 Lower front edge sticks out (pronounced belly)
67 Front edges overlap too much at the top
67 Front edges overlap too much at the bottom
68 Front is too short
68 Strong chest
69 Front opening sticks out
69 Armhole sticks out
70 Neckline is too close to the neck
70 Neckline is too far from the neck
71 Front pushes into the armhole
71 Armhole is cut out too far
72 Square shoulders
72 Sloping shoulders
73 Shoulders are too wide
73 Shoulders are too narrow
74 Armhole is too high
74 Armhole is too low
75 Back is too long
75 Back is too short

Tailoring the vest
76 Pressing a vest properly

The jacket
78 Sleeve before tailoring
80 Position of the shoulder pads
82 Stooped posture
84 Rounded back
86 S-shape posture
88 Erect posture
90 Jacket is too tight
91 Jacket is too loose
92 Seat is too tight
93 Seat is too loose
94 Rounded shoulders
95 Square shoulders
96 Sloping shoulders
97 One-sided sloping shoulder

The jacket

98 Shoulders are too narrow

99 Shoulders are too wide

100 Back is too long

101 Fold at the neck

102 Strong shoulder blades

103 Back fold does not roll up

104 Back width is too narrow

104 Back width is too wide

105 Make the jacket slimmer at the waist

106 Flat chest

107 Strong chest

108 Front part pushes into the armhole

109 Armhole is cut too wide
toward the front

110 Wrong width of scye

The jacket sleeve

112 Wrong sleeve pitch

112 Sleeve is too long at the back

113 Sleeve head is too flat

113 Sleeve head is too high

114 Imperfectly fitting sleeve

115 Tension on the sleeve and back

116 Width at the undersleeve

117 Sleeve hem is too tight

117 Sleeve hem is too wide

118 Armhole is too high

119 Armhole is too low

80 Strong upper arm

Neckline and collar of a jacket

122 Neckline is too narrow

123 Neckline is too wide

124 Collar is too low

125 Collar is too short

Tailoring the jacket

126 Pressing a jacket properly

127 Tips for tailoring

Appendix

128 Index

131 Abbreviations

132 Pattern alteration template

133 Measurement sheet

What is meant by the perfect fit?

The fit refers to the optimal way clothes suits the body. This may sound obvious, but it presents many challenges. Because in addition to different body dimensions, each person has their posture and individual body proportions.

Therefore, a ready-to-wear size sometimes has very little to do with an ideal fit. Classic ready-to-wear sizes are guidelines for the garments' length and width – they serve as a guide. After all, just because a garment is neither too tight nor too wide does not mean that it fits well.

Finding the cause of poor fit

This book examines the causes of poor fit and offers optimal solutions to the most common problems concerning the fit. Personal stylistic preferences are irrelevant in this context. Whether one tends towards the modern slim-fit shape or the classic wider cut, the garment should always fit with as few wrinkles as possible.

Identifying problems right from the start

Another challenge is the multitude of possibilities to achieve a perfect fit. It is rarely achieved with a single adjustment. Often the solution to a problem consists of a combination of several steps of modification. For the sake of convenience, the most common fitting errors are described individually on the following pages. Do not be afraid to combine specific improvements separately to achieve an even better result.

In most cases, it is advisable to work in the client's posture and proportions as early as the pattern-making stage. That spares tailors or sewists and customers from long and tedious fittings.

Achieving success with patience and perseverance

The more time you spend on the fit, the more you sharpen your eye for emerging problems. And the more causes you have discovered and eliminated, the easier it will be the next time. Have courage; practice makes perfect!

Good luck on your way to an ideal fit.

Taking measurements

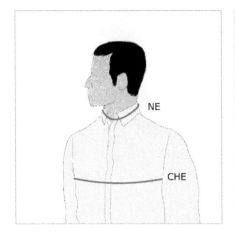

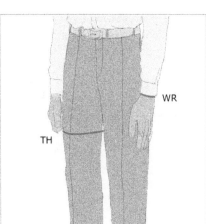

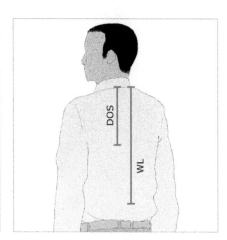

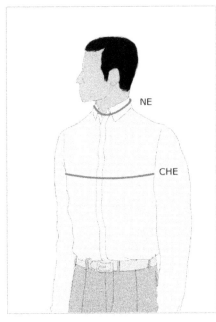

Taking measurements

Measurement sheet
You will find a sheet in the appendix on page 133.

Neck (*NE*)
When measuring the neck, care must be taken that the tape measure is not set too high. The circumference is measured at the base of the neck (on the skin), directly above the collarbone. It helps to keep two fingers between the tape measure and neck not to measure too narrow.

Chest (*CHE*)
When measuring the chest, the tape measure will be placed around the strongest chest point, then passed under the arms and slightly higher at the back.

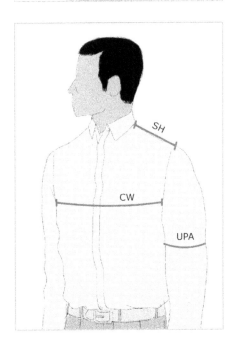

Waistline (*WAI*)
The waistline is measured exactly around the waist, at the narrowest point just above the hipbone. Here a waist measuring tape is fixed.

Waistband (*WB*)
The waistband is measured at the height of the desired position.

HIP
The hip width, or seat, is measured horizontally around the strongest point of the buttocks.

Shoulder width (*SH*)
The shoulder width is measured from the neckline to the shoulder bone.

Chest width (*CW*)
The chest width is measured across the strongest breast point from the left to the right arm.

Upper arm (*UPA*)
For muscular biceps, this measure is necessary. It is measured around the strongest point of the upper arm.

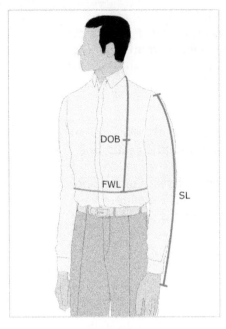

Sleeve length (*SL*)
Measure the sleeve length from the shoulder bone over a slightly bent elbow to about 2 cm above the first thumb joint.

Depth of brest (*DOB*)
The depth of the breast is measured from the 7th cervical vertebra across the shoulder to the front, to the point of the breast.
The 7th cervical vertebra is the vertebra protruding slightly at the back of the neck - in the pattern constructions, it is called the cervical-vertebra-point *CVP*.

Nape to front waist / Front waist length (*FWL*)
The front-waist-length is measured from the 7th cervical vertebra over the shoulder across the breast to the tape measure fixed at the waist.

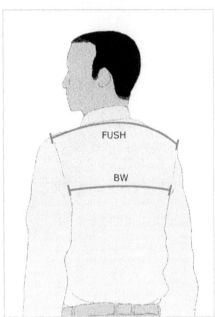

Full shoulder width (*FUSH*)
The full shoulder width is measured from the left shoulder bone, across the back to the right shoulder bone.

Back width (*BW*)
It is measured across the back in a relaxed position, from the left to the right arm.

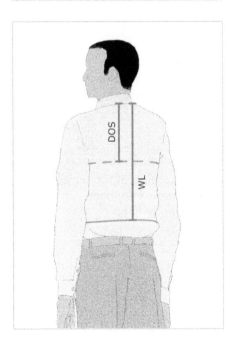

Depth of Scye /
Depth of armhole (*DOS*)
To measure the depth of scye, push a piece of cardboard under the customer's arm and measure from the 7th cervical vertebra along the middle of the back to the cardboard's upper edge.

Nape to waistline / Waist length (*WL*)
The waist's length is measured from the 7th cervical vertebra along the middle of the back to the tape measure fixed at the waistline.

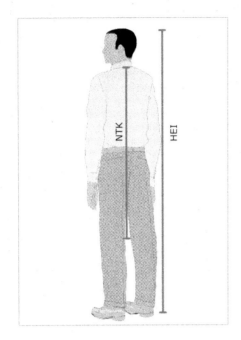

Height (*HEI*)

Mostly, the customer knows his height. If you do not trust this information, it is measured from the top of the head to the sole, preferably without shoes. Otherwise, subtract the heel height.

Nape to knee (*NTK*)

The nape-to-knee is measured from the 7th cervical vertebra along the mid-back across the seat to the knee.

The 7th cervical vertebra is the vertebra protruding slightly at the back of the neck - in the pattern constructions, it is called the cervical-vertebra-point *CVP*.

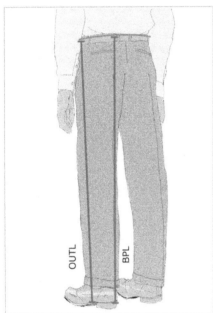

Back pants length (*BPL*)

First, fix the tape measure at the point where the waistband should sit. Now the back pants length is measured from the waistband to the floor.
(If the customer is wearing shoes, measure to the top of the heel.)

Outside leg (*OUTL*)

First, fix the tape measure at the point where the waistband should sit.
Now the outside leg can be measured on the side from the waistband down to the floor.
(If the customer is wearing shoes, measure to the top of the heel.)

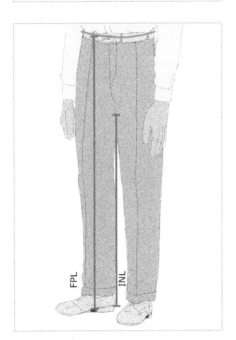

Inside leg (*INL*)

To measure the inside leg, have the customer pull up the pants into the crotch. Then it is easy to determine the measurement on the legs' inside from the crotch to the floor. (If the customer wears shoes, the heel height is subtracted.)

Front pants length (*FPL*)

First, fix a tape measure at the point where the waistband should sit. Now the front length of the pants is measured from the waistband down to the floor. (If the customer wears shoes, the heel height is subtracted.)

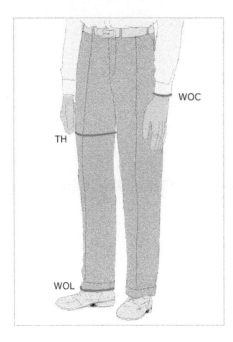

Thigh (*TH*)
The thigh circumference is measured around the thigh's strongest point, about 10 cm below the crotch.

Width of length (*WOL*)
The hem circumference is measured at the bottom of the trouser hem according to the customer requirements.

Width of cuffs (*WOC*)
The width of the cuff is measured around the wrist, directly at the base of the hand. If the customer always wears a watch, this must be taken into account on one side.

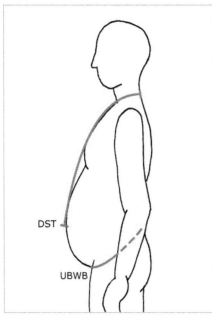

Depth of stomach (DST)
The depth of the stomach is measured from the 7th cervical vertebra (see explanation *NTK*, p. 12), over the shoulder across the front, to the strongest point on the stomach. Since there are different belly shapes, such as a high stomach, pointed, or hanging belly, this measurement is essential for a perfect fit.

Under belly waistband (*UBW*B)
If the customer wears their trousers below the stomach, this measurement is incredibly important and is also used as the low waistline.

Attention:
The front pants length and the later zipper of the trousers are remarkably short in trousers that sit below the belly.

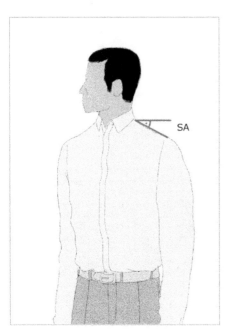

Shoulder angle *(SA)*
The shoulder angle can be determined easily with the mobile phone and a protractor app. The device is placed on the shoulder at the base of the neck. This makes it easier to classify a hanging shoulder. It is best to measure directly with the desired shoulder pad.

Approximate shoulder angles
Square	*approx. 10° - 16°*
Half square	*approx. 16° - 21°*
Normal	*approx. 21° - 25°*
Half sloping	*approx. 25° - 30°*
Sloping	*approx. 30° - 36°*

Taken measurements in a proportional pattern

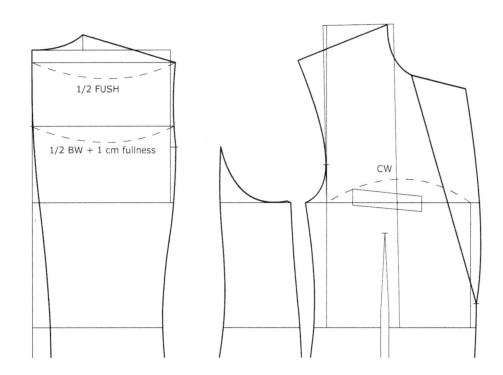

1/2 FUSH

1/2 BW + 1 cm fullness

CW

Taken measurements in the pattern

For a modern proportional pattern, you don't need too many measurements. Usually, you can get along with *HEI*, *NE*, *CHE*, *WAI*, *HIP*, and *SL*. With these, you can create a decent pattern.

Especially as a beginner, you cannot make too many mistakes and learn how to create a pattern. Slight deviations in build or posture can be altered in fittings.

It only becomes complicated when a body deviates from the "ideal" proportions. In this case, additional measurements must be added to the pattern. However, one should always compare the taken measurements with the calculated proportion measurements. Excessive deviations are noticeable and must be taken into account to avoid errors. In this case, you should at least be skeptical. But of course, more enormous differences are also possible.

It is especially important to trust the person taking the measurements. A photo of the customer can provide additional assurance that the measurements are correct.
The taken length measurements for the jacket (*DOS*, *WL*, *DOB*, *FWL*, *DST*), are naturally used for a vest or coat, as well. The width measurements must be determined separately.

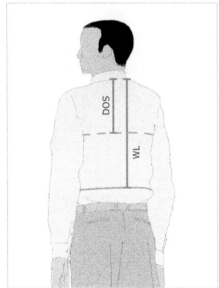

Depth of scye (*DOS*)

The depth of scye is also the chest line. It generally defines the height of the armhole. When in doubt, the armhole should be a little higher. You can always cut it out later.

Waist length (*WL*)

When it comes to the waist length, you should always compare the taken measurement with the calculated one. If the two don't differ too much, an average of the two numbers is a good reference point. This maintains the "ideal" proportions and a balanced appearance.

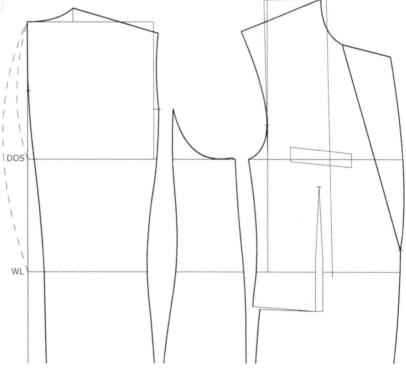

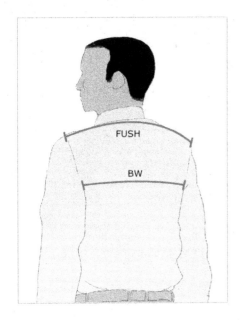

Full shoulder (*FUSH*)

If you notice that the customer has square shoulders, this should be included in the pattern. In most cases, the back width BW is also affected by this. The easiest way is to mark half the measurement on the shoulder in the pattern. The transition from a wide shoulder to a small chest is not that easy. There are no fixed rules for this; you have to approach it step by step and try it out.

Back width (*BW*)

Strong shoulder blades or a muscular build can influence this measurement. Therefore, it is helpful to check the back width = 1/2 *BW* + 1 cm fullness.

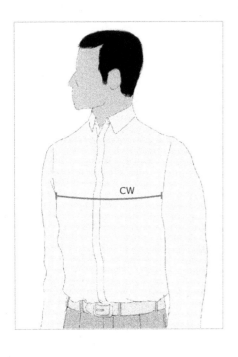
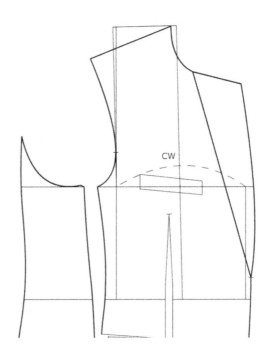

Chest width (*CW*)

A strong chest or physique can affect this measure. Therefore, it is recommended to check the chest width = 1/2 *CW* + 1 cm fullness.

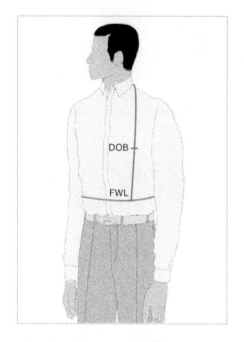
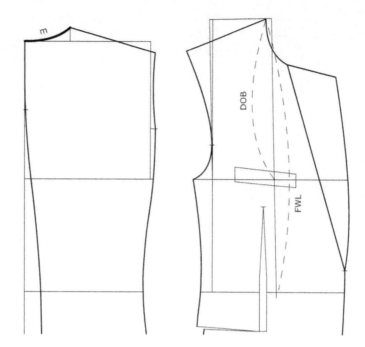

Depth of breast (*DOB*)

The position of the depth of the breast is crucial for tailoring. With this measure, the breast's position can be pressed at the correct place (ironed into shape), and the canvas receives the darts in the right places for its shape. As the depth of the breast is measured from the 7th cervical vertebra, it is essential to measure the back neckline (*m*) and subtract it from the measurement (any seam allowances must be taken into account).

Front waist lenght (*FWL*)

In case of a strong chest, rounded back or upright posture, this measurement is of interest.
As with the depth of breast, it is essential to subtract that part from the back neckline (consider seam allowances).

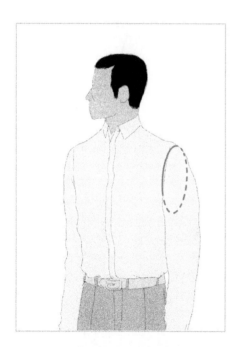
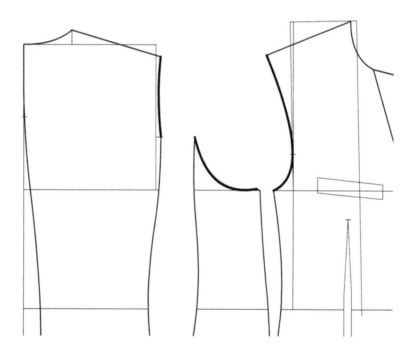

Circumference of scye (*COS*)

A strong chest, a muscular physique, or strong upper arms can influence the armhole circumference. Measured loosely around the base of the arm, this gives a clue to the finished armhole circumference. This can avoid an armhole that is too small but above all, too large. The rule of thumb is roughly: *COS* = 1/2 *CHE* (+/- 2 cm). Pay attention to seam allowances when measuring.

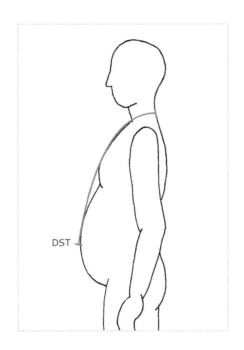

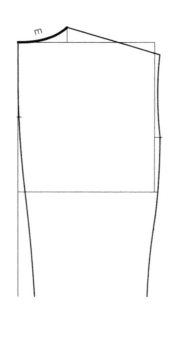

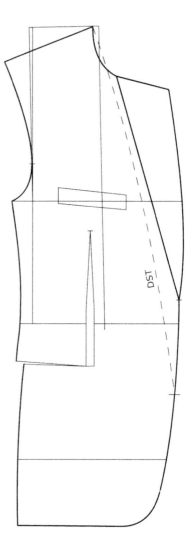

Depth of stomach (*DST*)

The depth of stomach is similar to the depth of breast, it is important for making the pattern and, above all, for tailoring. With this measure, the stomach can be pressed in at the right place (ironed into shape), and the canvas receives the darts in the correct positions for its form.

It is also essential to subtract the back neckline; any seam allowances must be considered (see also the explanation for *DOB* and *FWL* on page 17).

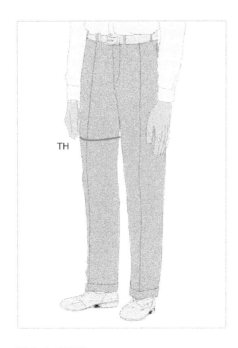

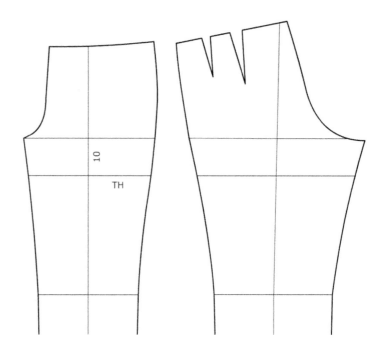

Thigh (*TH)*

For narrow pants without waistband pleats, this measurement should be checked and adjusted in the pattern. Especially when sitting down, the pants can otherwise become too tight at the thigh. Sensitive fabrics with cashmere components will wear away quickly on muscular thighs if it is too tight at this point. The thigh width is marked approx. 10 cm below the crotch line. An extra width of approx. 3 cm is ideal here.

Body shape and posture

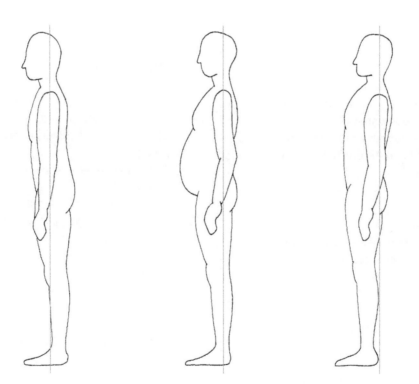

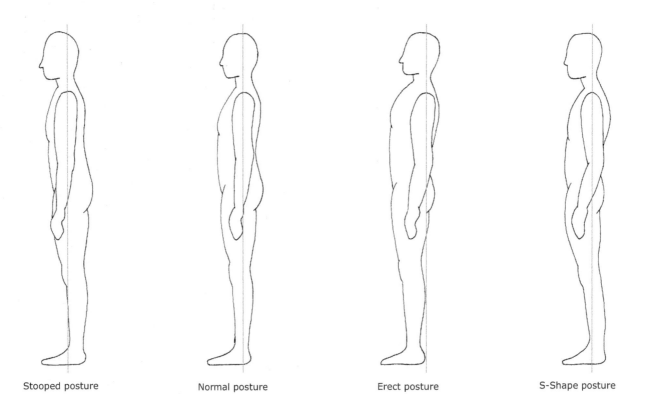

Stooped posture   Normal posture   Erect posture   S-Shape posture

Basic types of posture

Each customer can be matched to one of the four basic postures. Besides, there may be further peculiarities in the body shape.

The shoulders' position and thus the sleeve pitch (arm position) is also different for each person and has to be considered.

Stooped posture

- The person puts their weight on the forefoot.
- The upper body is bent forward.
- Shoulders often come forward
  (see shoulders on p. 79).
- Arms go forward
  (see arm position on p. 78).

Normal posture

- The person stands with their weight in the middle of their foot.
- head, shoulders, waist, and hips are exactly aligned.

Erect posture

- The person puts their weight on their heel.
- The upper body (the chest) is directed upwards.
- The head often points upwards as well.
- Shoulders are frequently pulled backward
  (see p. 79).
- Arms are pulled backward
  (see p. 78).
- Knees are mostly straight.
- The depth of breast should be measured.

S-Shape

- The person stands with the weight in the middle of the foot.
- The pelvis (the hips) is tilted forward.
- The back is somewhat round.
- The head is firmly pointed forward (turtle neck).

Combinations

Often several aspects of posture or body shape come together.

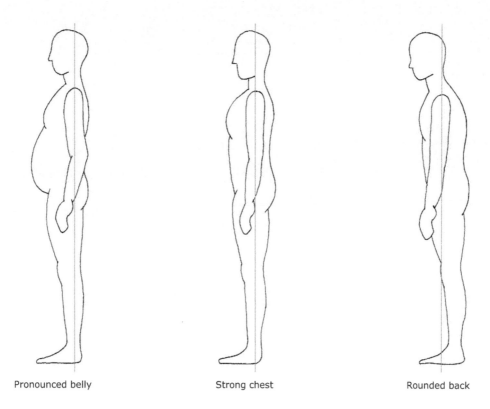

Pronounced belly   Strong chest   Rounded back

Common body shapes

Along with the posture, the customer's body shape should also be taken into account. There may be other unique features such as narrow or wide hips, strong upper arms or thighs, and asymmetry in the shoulders. Therefore it is especially important to pay attention to this when taking measurements and to note everything or take a photo.

Pronounced belly

- The person puts their weight on their heel.
- The upper body is leaning backward to balance the weight.
- Shoulders are often pulled backward as well (see p. 79).
- Arms are pulled backward (see p. 78).
- Knees are mostly straight.
- The depth of stomach should be measured.

Strong chest

- A strong chest is very similar to an erect posture, but in this case, the person is standing up straight.
- Either the muscles are heavily toned or the chest is arched due to lung training (e.g., diving, singing or brass band music).
- The depth of breast should be measured.

Rounded back

- A rounded back is very similar to a stooped posture.
- The upper body slightly slumps and is therefore tilted forward.
- Shoulders often go forward (see p. 79).
- Arms go forward (see p. 78).
- Sometimes, the knees are slightly bent.
- A rounded back and a stooped posture go together often.

Short or tall size

Everybody shape and posture can, of course, also come in short or tall sizes. The correct proportions of the garment are obtained by measuring the body height precisely.

Working it into the pattern

When drawing a proportional pattern, it is necessary to adapt the pattern to the customer's shape and posture.

With much practice, this can be done while drawing. However, it is easier if the basic pattern is drawn first, and then the changes are worked in after that.

Fit and fitting

 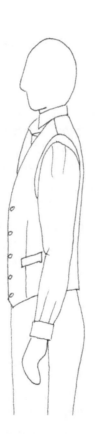 

Example for fitting a jacket

The jacket is pulled over evenly at the front so that the center front's stitches are exactly one above the other. The waistline must now meet exactly.

When pinning the jacket together, any tension should be avoided, and e.g., an excessive back width should not be pulled forward. This would mean that a false balance would be mistakenly assumed.

Put the front parts together loosely, but not too loose or too tight. Existing ease in the back or on the side will be pinned tighter during the fitting process.

Checking the sleeve pitch

If the jacket is correctly pinned together at the front, the sleeves' fit is adjusted from the side.

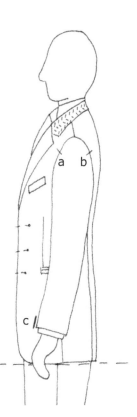

On the sleeve, the notches are marked on the sleeve head and the front (*a*) and back (*b*) with chalk. A well-fitting sleeve may have some length at the back seam. This makes it more comfortable. However, it must fit without tension in the front. At the front of the wrist, the sleeve should not protrude from the shirt cuff. The sleeve pitch is now marked below the pocket opening (*c*).

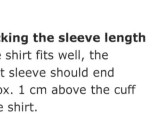

Checking the sleeve length

If the shirt fits well, the jacket sleeve should end approx. 1 cm above the cuff of the shirt.

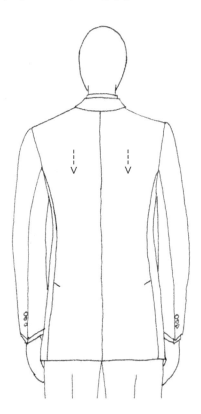

Smoothing out the back

Since there is usually no lining worked in for the first fitting, the fabric can get caught on the upper back, or "stick". Therefore the back is smoothed out from the shoulders down. In this way, you can detect if the back is too short or too long. Use both hands at the same time while smoothing, so that both sides sit evenly.
Now the sleeves and the undercollar are removed. This makes it easier to adjust the front and back.

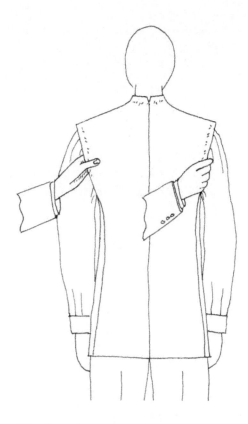

Aligning the upper back
Now hold the back at armhole level with both hands and place the back seam precisely in the center of the body. Then smooth out the back shoulder area again.

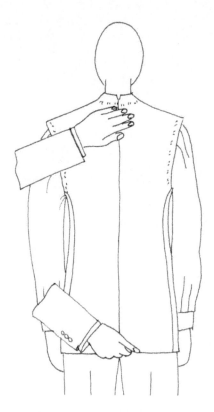

Aligning the lower back
Next, the neck area is held in place with a flat hand, while the other hand is used to catch the back hem and easily move it into the correct position.

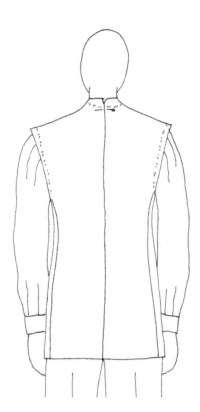

Securing the back
The back part is now attached to the shirt below the collar line with a pin.

Aligning the front part
Check the position of the front shoulder area as well. Then, the left shoulders seam is opened.

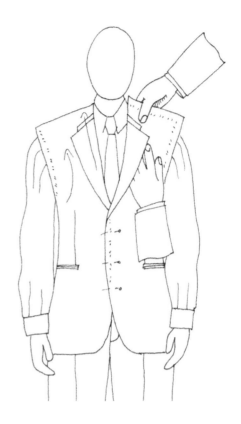

Adjusting the front shoulder
The left hand fixes the front edge at the waist so that the jacket is not pulled up unintentionally. With the right hand, the shoulder area is placed, more or less to the neck, depending on the balance.

Smoothing out the chest
Hold the left front in your right hand and keep it at this position. With your left hand, smooth out the chest from the armhole and move to the shoulder in a curve. The front piece must not slide up or down at this point.

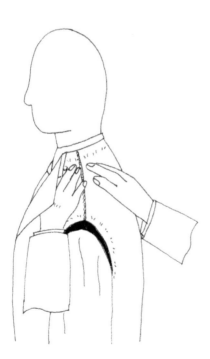

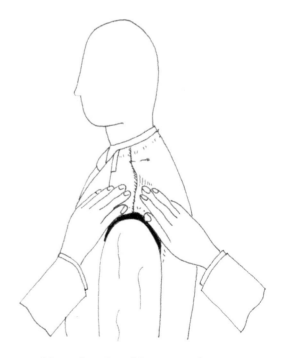

Attaching the shoulder, part 1
Your left hand rests on the front part and holds it in place. With your right hand, carefully smooth out the back from the center to the front and, avoiding tension, pin it to the front shoulder about 3 cm from the neck hole.

Attaching the shoulder, part 2
The back should fit snugly at the back armhole; this creates a certain width at the back shoulder seam (only as much as can be shrinked due to ironing into form). A pin is now placed on the outer shoulder.

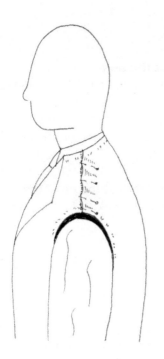

Pinning the shoulder

If necessary, remove the basting stitches that are securing the shoulder pad and move the pad to the correct position (see shoulder pads on p. 79). Then the width is evenly arranged at the back shoulder seam and pinned. Finally, the shoulder seam is pinned right at the neckline without creating any tension at the collar.

When the shoulder seam is pinned together, there should still be enough space at the outside between the shoulder pad and the shoulder to allow two fingers to slide under.

Balance control

Afterward, the right shoulder seam is pinned neatly as well. When the pins at the front center are removed, the edges remain vertical with proper balance. This check should be performed in any case. The lengths of the two front parts must not be unequal now.

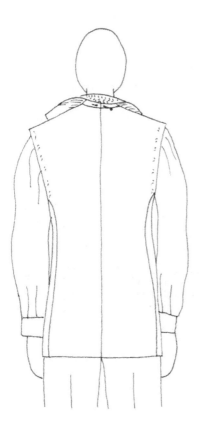

Attaching the collar

Now that both shoulders have adequately been pinned, the pin that was attached to secure the back can now be removed.

The center back should be marked on the undercollar. Then attach the undercollar to the middle of the back so that approx. 1 - 1.5 cm of the shirt collar are visible (a proper shirt collar is required). If the collar stand is too low, the crease can be moved upwards slightly.

Now pin the collar in place up to the shoulder seam while avoiding tension.

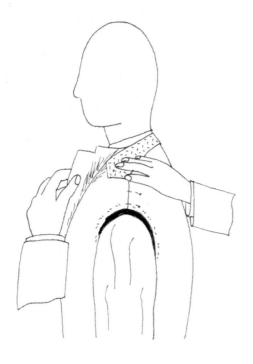

The collar position at the side

At the shoulder seam the collar must be positioned correctly as well. The collar break should merge homogeneously into the lapel break, otherwise the collar break has to be moved inward or outward as far as necessary.

There must be enough length at the tip of the shoulder so that no tension wrinkles form under the collar.

The right part of the collar is attached in the same way. Now the lapel is folded at the lapel break and attached to the undercollar.

Finally, the width and the height of the lapel can be marked. Although this has nothing to do with the fit, it contributes significantly to the silhouette of the jacket.

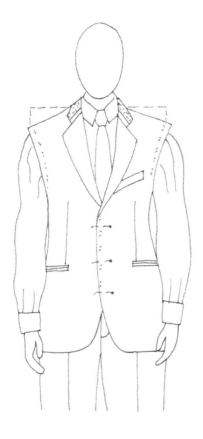

The shoulder width

The shoulder width also depends on style aspects, but it is always determined according to the customer's wishes (of course, you can intervene with advice). The type of tailoring also influences the width of the shoulders.

As a guideline, you can say: The less shoulder padding and the lighter the construction (less and thinner horsehair interlining), the narrower the shoulders can become.

Before the shoulder width is marked, the jacket is pinned together again at the center front.

The fit of the jacket

The jacket should fit loosely. The shoulder width, i.e., the sleeve seam, must extend at least to the shoulder bone. If you do not move, the jacket lies flat and does not create any folds or wrinkles. There should be enough room for natural movement.

  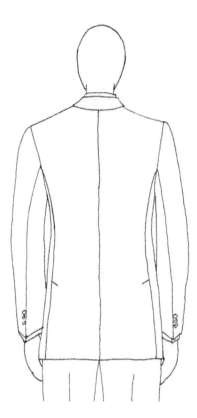

- The shoulder width extends exactly to the shoulder bone.
- The upper arms should not show through the sleeve.
- The classic length of the jacket extends to the beginning of the fingers when the arms are lowered. For extra long or short arms, proportional measurements should be used (approx. 1/8 *HEI* x 3.5).

- The shirt cuff lies exactly at the wrist. The sleeve length of the jacket is about 1 cm shorter than the length of the cuff of the shirt (a suitable shirt is a required for this).
- There should not be any diagonal pulls on the sleeve.
- The front part is about 1 cm longer than the back.

- The back sits smoothly.
- Slits fall evenly.
- At the back of the neck, the shirt collar should be visible by about 1 cm.
- At the shoulder blades, a jacket needs some extra width, so the arms can be moved forward comfortably.

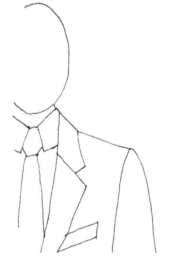

- The jacket collar sits loosely but without any space around the entire shirt collar.
- At the side of the neck, the shirt collar should be visible by about 1 cm.

The fit of the vest

The fitting of the vest is the same as with a jacket or coat. If there is no movement, the vest fits smooth and does not form any folds or wrinkles. There should be enough room for natural movement.

 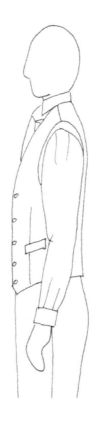 

- The shoulder width of a vest is about 3 - 4 cm narrower than the natural shoulder.
- With a well-fitting shirt, the armhole of the vest should be approximately at the same level as the armhole of the shirt.
- At the center front, the length of the vest should protrude approx. 4 cm above the waistband.

- The armhole is just large enough to allow free movement.
- The entire armhole sits close to the body.
- The front part is longer than the back.
- The waistband is completely covered.

- The back sits smoothly.
- With the belt in the waist you can tighten the vest by about 4 cm.
- At the back of the neck, the vest should come up to the neckline of the shirt collar.
- The back length should cover the waistband by approx. 2 cm.

- The opening fits loosely all around and closely to the shirt collar.

The fit of the pants

The pants should be tight in the waistband but loose around the legs. Pants that are too tight are uncomfortable, appear like leggings, and look rather embarrassing for most figures. If you do not move, the pants are smooth and do not form any folds or wrinkles (apart from the fold at the crease). There should be enough room for natural movement. The waistband should be high enough so that buttocks will not stick out when sitting down (plumber's smile).

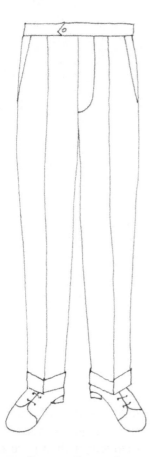
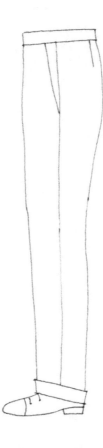
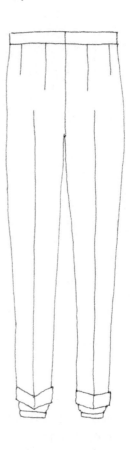

- Depending on the customer's wishes, the waistband is positioned at the waist or slightly lower, above the hip bone.
- The waistband is not too tight (some customers with a pronounced belly like the feeling of constriction in pants that sit beneath the belly).
- The crotch area is roomy enough for a relaxed feeling.

- Due to anatomy, the waistband is somewhat lower in the front than in the back.
- No wrinkles are forming under the seat. A slight horizontal fold for freedom of movement (normal walking) is fine.
- The front trousers can be a little too long at the hem and lie on the shoe. This can form a slight fold.

- The back of the pants is smooth.
- The hem ends approximately at the heel of the shoe.
- With a slim pant leg, the pants are slightly shorter than with a wide pant leg.

Fitting the pants

First, the waistband is placed in the appropriate place according to the customer's wishes (tighten or loosen the waistband as required). Next, the balance between right/left (see page 38) and front/back (see pages 34/35) is adjusted. To adjust the balance, pin the length below the waistband as required. Hips that are too strong or thighs that are too loose are pinned tighter.

Anything that is too tight should be noted and expanded later.

Therefore, each finished measurement of the pants should be compared with the taken measurements before trying them on. Pants being too loose are always better than ones that are too tight. There is no point in undoing the outside or inside seam during the fitting and pinning them back together.

The fit of the shirt

The shirt fits loosely at the body. Even with a slim-fit shirt, there should still be air between the body and the fabric. Otherwise, a straight cut might be more suitable.

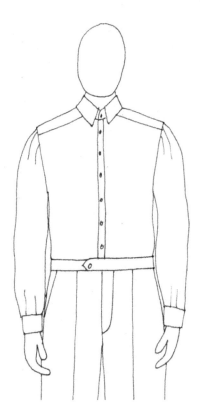  

- The shoulder width extends to the shoulder bone.
- The length is generously measured (at least down to the strongest part of the seat), so that the shirt does not slip out of the pants when moving.
- The armhole is not cut out too low.

- The entire armhole sits close to the body.
- The cuff of the shirt lies exactly on the wrist.
- A turn-up cuff should not be too large. Otherwise, the jacket sleeve will also be too wide.

- For more freedom of movement the sleeve length is approx. 3 - 4 cm longer than necessary.
- The back sits smoothly.

- The shirt collar is neither too wide nor too tight (two fingers should fit between the neck and the collar).
- The collar turn-up looks even and smooth.

Fitting errors at the pants

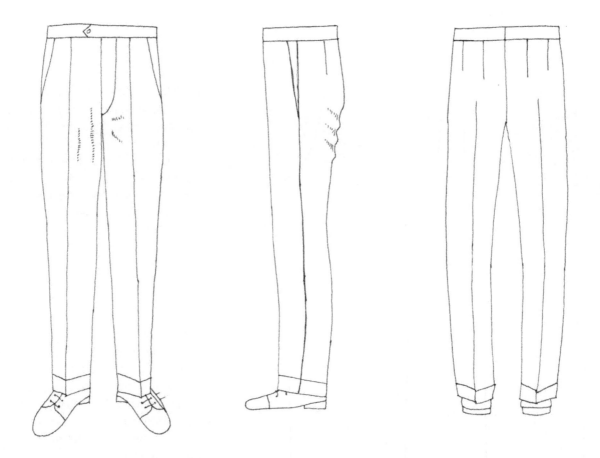

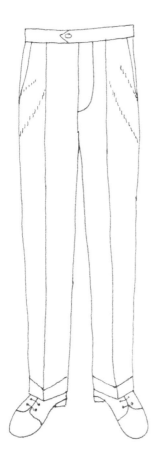

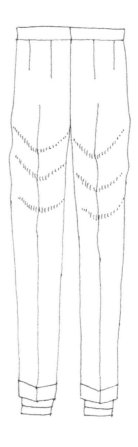

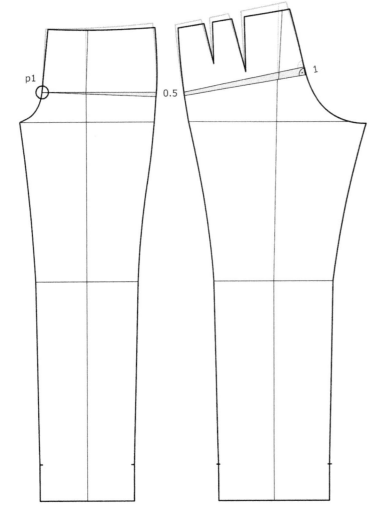

Pelvis tilted forward
- The pelvis tilted forward can be found, for example, in an S-shaped posture.
- There is too much length at the back of the pants.
- When viewed from the side, creases form from the upper front to the lower back.

Changes to the pattern
- The side seam of the front is put together by approx. 0.5 cm using the pivot point *p1*.
- The back is put together accordingly (0.5 cm at the side seam and approx. 1 cm at the seat seam).
- The shape of the side seam should be balanced.
- The shape of the seat seam should be balanced.

Note
Most likely, the alteration for a flat seat must also be considered (see p. 46).

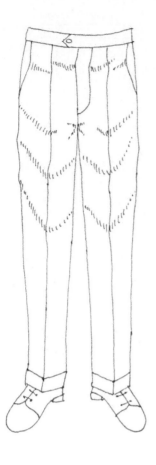
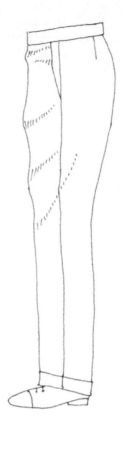
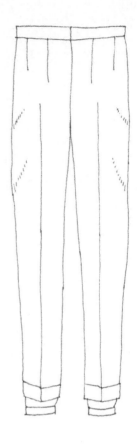

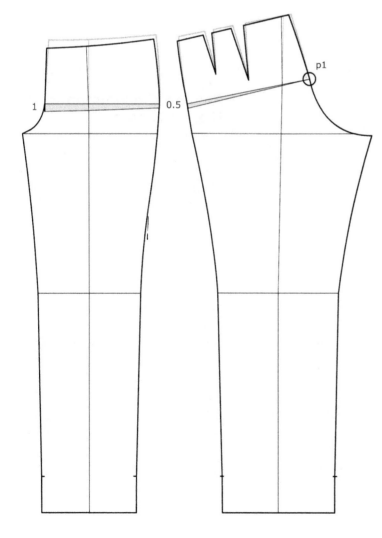

Pelvis tilted backward (hollow back)

- A pelvis tilted backward can be found in people with pronounced bellies or hollow backs.
- There is too much length at the front trousers.
- When viewed from the side, creases form from the upper back to the lower front.

Changes to the pattern

- Using the pivot point *p1*, the side seam at the back is put together by approx. 0.5 cm.
- The front is put together accordingly (0.5 cm at the side seam and approx. 1 cm at the fly).
- The shape of the side seam should be balanced.
- The shape of the fly seam should be balanced.

Note

Most likely, the alteration for a strong seat must also be considered (see p. 47).

35

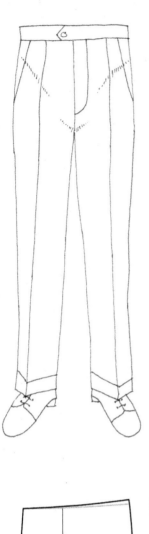
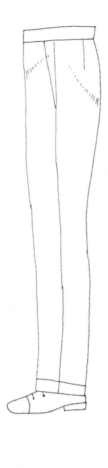
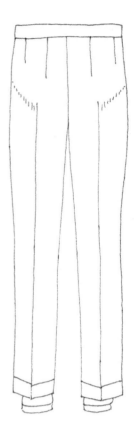

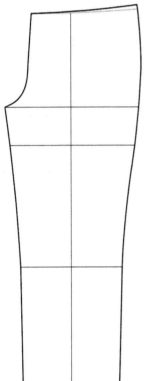
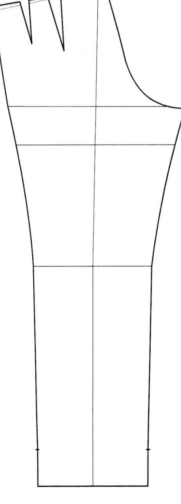

Raising the waistband at the side seam

- Diagonal creases form from the front crotch point upward and outward toward the waistband.
- From the back crotch point, creases form upward and outward toward the waistband.
- When viewed from the side, the side seam indicates an upward pull.

Changes to the pattern

- The waistline is raised at the front and back by the required measurement (approx. 0.5 cm).

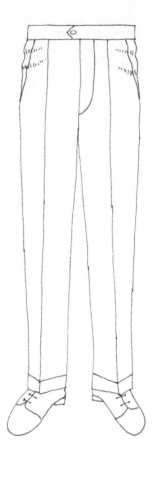
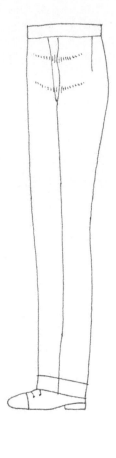
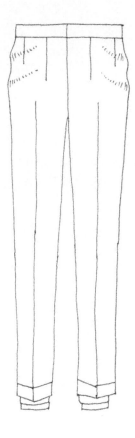

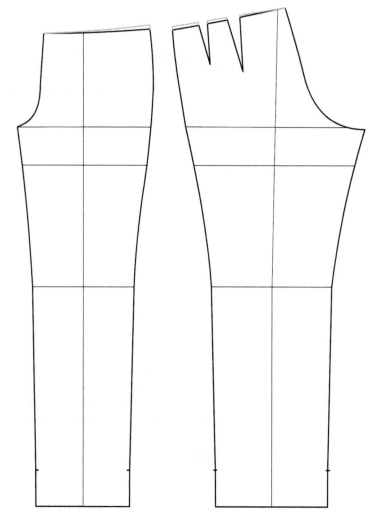

Lowering the waistband at the side seam

- Creases are formed at the side seam at the front and back. The extra length is obvious.
- When the extra length is pinned with needles, the pants are flat and smooth.

Changes to the pattern

- The waistline is marked lower on the front and back by the required measurement (approx. 0.5 cm).

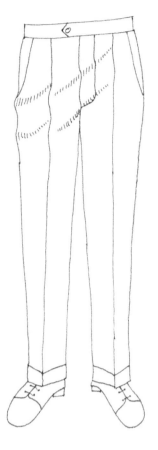
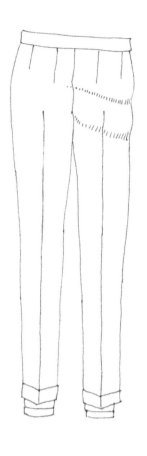

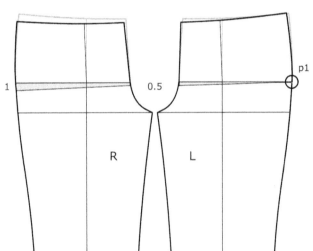

Pelvis tilted sideways

- The pelvis is tilted to one side because, for example, one leg is shorter.
- A tilted pelvis changes the entire posture of the upper body.

Changes to the pattern

The front
- Both front parts of the pants are placed side by side first.
- Using the pivot point *p1*, the side seam at the drooping side is put together by approx. 1 cm (approx. 0.5 cm at the fly).

The back
- Both back parts of the pants are placed side by side first.
- Using the pivot point *p2*, the side seam at the drooping side is put together by approx. 1 cm (approx. 0.5 cm at the seat seam).

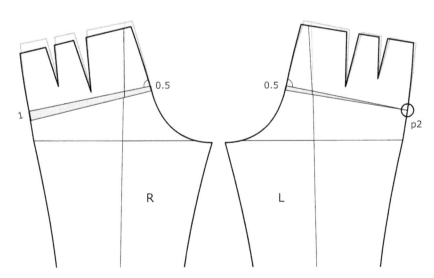

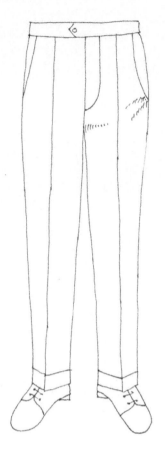

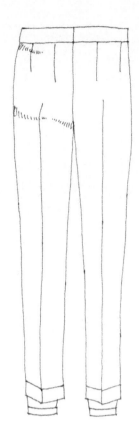

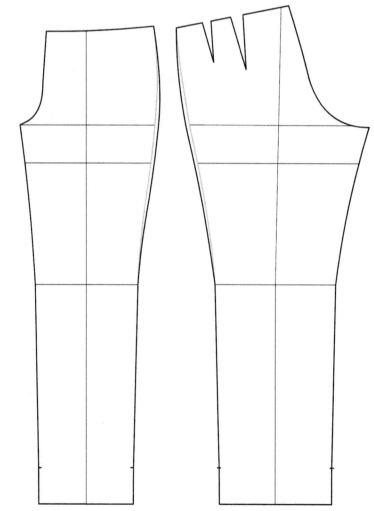

The hip is stronger on one side

- The pocket on one side of the front opens.
- Tension wrinkles that run crosswise are created.

Changes to the pattern

The front
- The hip curve is drawn wider on the corresponding side (by approx. 0.5 cm)

The back
- The hip curve is drawn wider on the corresponding side (by approx. 0.5 cm)

Note
This change is made on one side only.

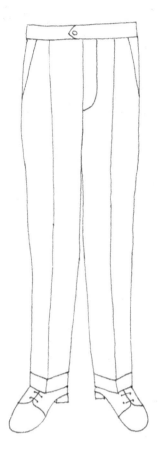
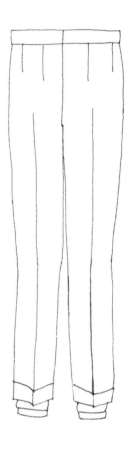

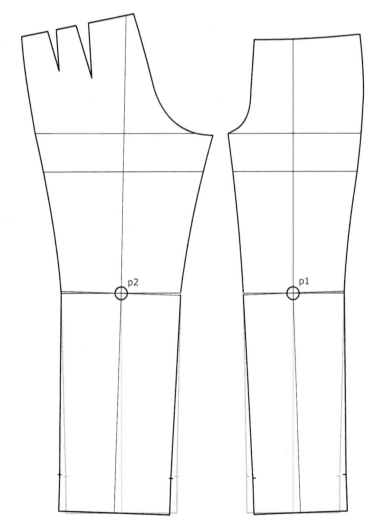

Knock-knees
- The legs curve inward so that the feet are apart when the knees are touching.

Changes to the pattern
The front
- Using the pivot point *p1*, the lower part of the front is turned outwards by approx. 1 cm.

The back
- Using the pivot point *p2*, the lower part of the back is turned outwards by approx. 1 cm.

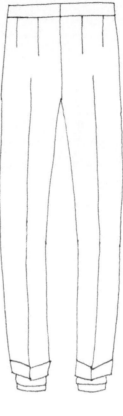

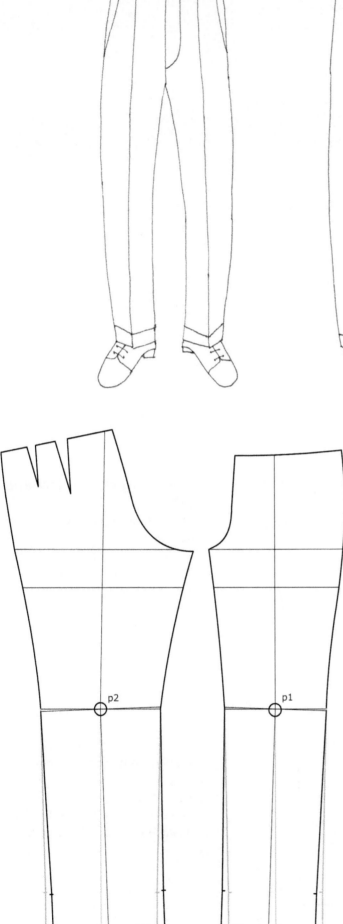

Bowlegs
- The legs that curve outward at the knee; bandy legs.

Changes to the pattern
The front
- Using the pivot point *p1*, the lower part of the front is turned inwards by approx. 1 cm.

The back
- Using the pivot point *p2*, the lower part of the back is turned inwards by approx. 1 cm.

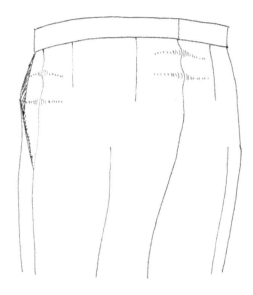

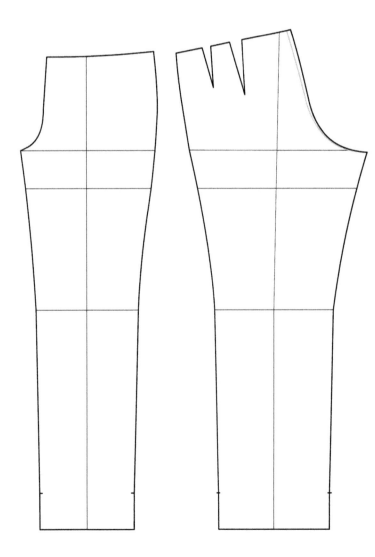

Extending the waistband width

- The waistband is very tight and ties up
- At the center back, this tension causes horizontal wrinkles.
- The front pockets are pulled open.

Changes to the pattern

- At the back part of the pants, the center back is extended.
- The side seams may also have to be extended.

Note

It may also be necessary to consider the alterations for a strong seat (see p. 47) and a strong hip curve (see p. 44).
If the extension exceeds 4 cm, it is advisable to extend the side seams as well.

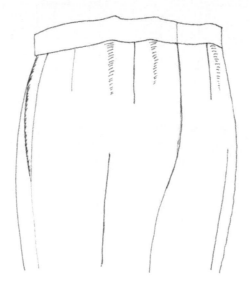

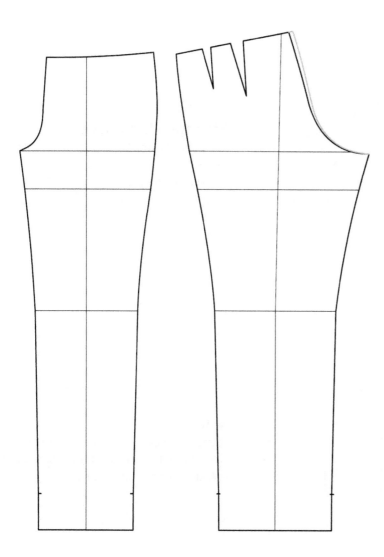

Reducing the waistband width

- The waistband is very loose and does not stay in the desired position.
- This causes vertical creases at the back center.

Changes to the pattern

- On the back of the trousers, the center back is drawn tighter.
- The side seams may also have to be tighter.

Note

It may also be necessary to consider the alterations for a flat seat
(see p. 46) and a less pronounced hip curve (see p. 45).
If the reduction exceeds 4 cm, it is advisable to make the side seams tighter as well.

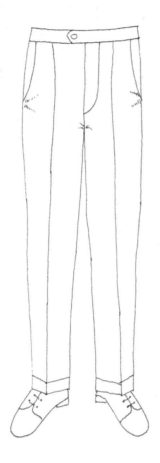

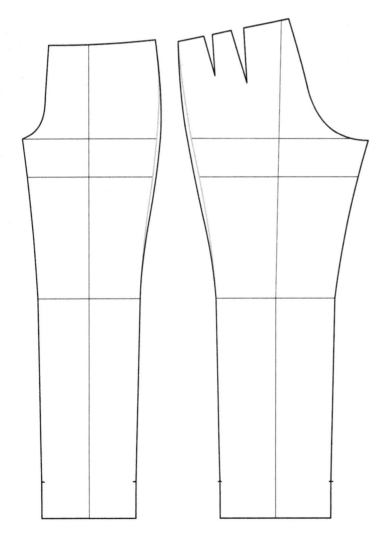

Stronger hip curve

- Horizontal wrinkles form around the hips.
- The front pockets open.
- Horizontal wrinkles form around the seat.

Changes to the pattern

The front
- The hip curve is drawn wider by approx. 0.5 cm.

The back
- The hip curve is drawn wider by approx. 0.5 cm.

Note

It may be necessary to consider the alterations for raising the waistband at the side seam (see p. 36).

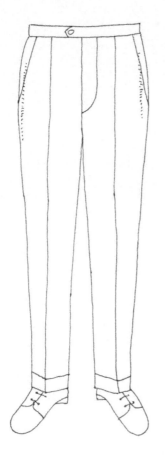

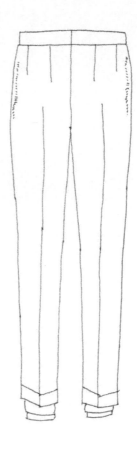

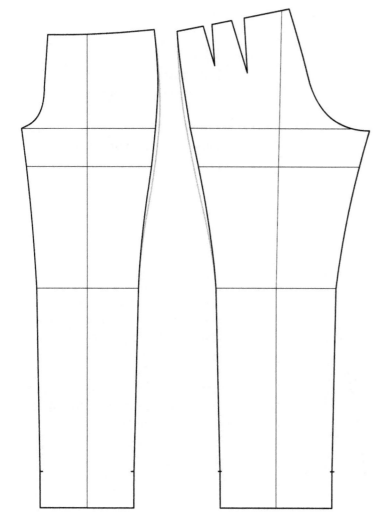

Less pronounced hip curve
- Vertical creases form around the hips.
- Vertical creases form around the seat.

Changes to the pattern
The front
- The hip curve is drawn flatter by approx. 0.5 cm.

The back
- The hip curve is drawn flatter by approx. 0.5 cm.

Note
It may be necessary to consider the alterations for lowering the waistband at the side seam (see p. 37).

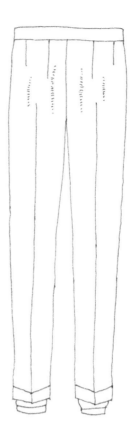

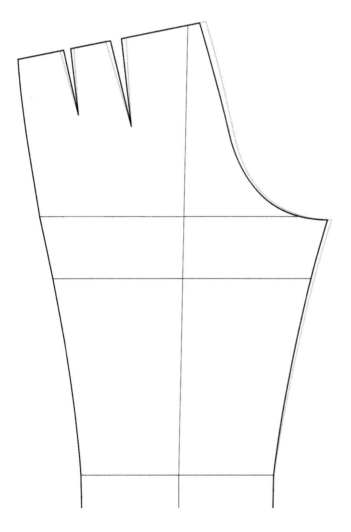

Flat seat
- Vertical creases form around the
  seat.
- The back part of the pants obviously
  consists of too much material.

Changes to the pattern
- At the back part of the pants, the
  seat seam is drawn narrower bay
  approx. 1 cm.
- The tip of the inside seam (the
  crotch) is drawn narrower.
- The darts are drawn less deep.
  The width of the waistband should
  be the same as before.

Note
It may also be necessary to consider
the alterations for the pelvic tilted
forward (see page 34).

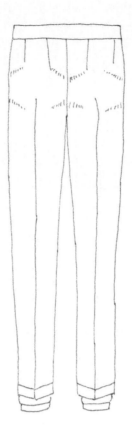

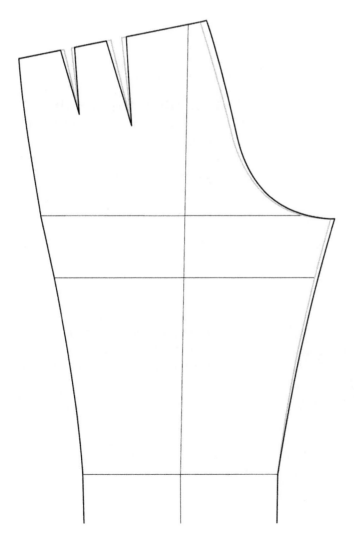

Strong seat

- Horizontal wrinkles form around the seat.
- The back part of the pants obviously consists of too little material.

Changes to the pattern

- At the back part of the pants, the seat seam is drawn wider by approx. 1 cm.
- The tip of the inside seam (the crotch) is drawn wider.
- The darts are drawn deeper. The width of the waistband should be the same as before.

Note

It may also be necessary to consider the alterations for the pelvic tilted backward (see page 35).

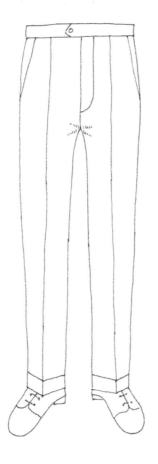

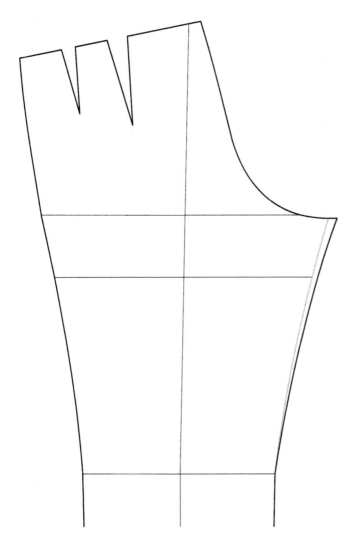

Extending the crotch
- Wrinkles form at the crotch in the front.
- The front part of the pants is pulled inwards at the top of the inside seam.
- Wrinkles form at the crotch in the back.
- The back part of the pants is pulled inwards at the top of the inside seam.

Changes to the pattern
- The back crotch is drawn larger (approx. 1 - 2 cm).
- This will smooth out the wrinkles.

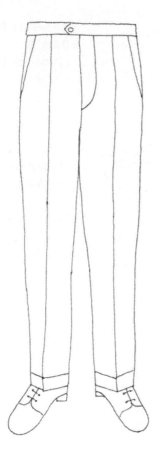
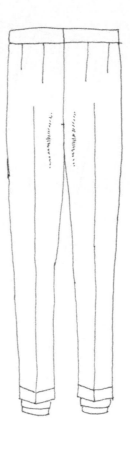

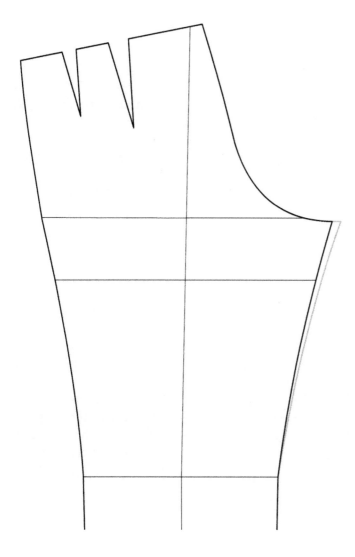

Reducing the crotch
- Vertical creases form below the seat
  on the back part of the pants.

Changes to the pattern
- The back crotch is drawn narrower
  (approx. 1 - 2 cm).

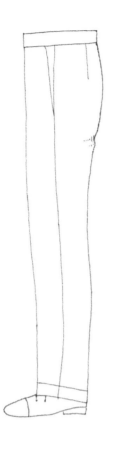

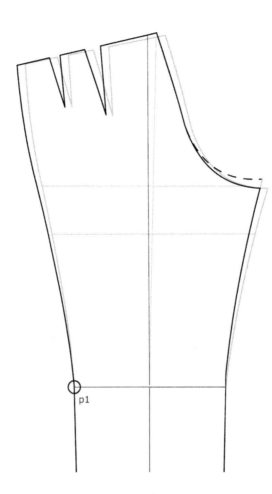

Ease at the back of the pants

- A pair of pants need a little length at the back, under the seat.
- As a result, the trousers do not constrict when sitting, and there is not too much pressure on the thigh when walking.

Changes to the pattern

- If there is not enough length in the back, the upper part of the pants is turned outward by approx. 1 - 2 cm using the pivot point *p1*.
- The length of the inside seam must be adjusted lower so that it fits to the front part of the pants again.

Note

In pattern drafting, this is also called the "inclination" of the back of the pants.

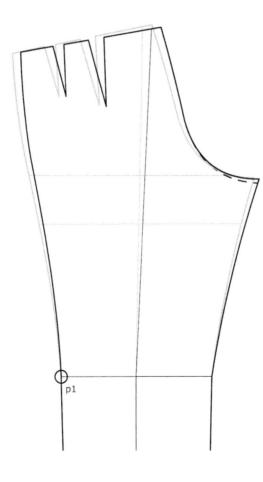

Too much room in the back

- There are limits to the comfortable length of the back.
- However, for customers who sit a lot, it is more comfortable to have more length.

Changes to the pattern

- If there is too much length in the back part of the pants, the top part of the pattern is turned to the right by approx. 1 - 2 cm using the pivot point *p1*.
- The length of the inside seam must be adjusted lower so that it fits to the front part of the pants again.

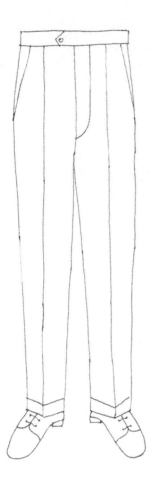

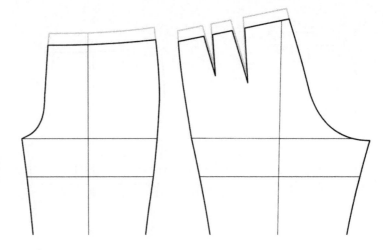

Lowering the rise
- The waistband is too high.
- The pants look very old-fashioned.

Changes to the pattern
The front
- The waistband line is drawn down by approx. 1 - 2 cm, parallel to the previous one.
- The width of the waistband at the front must be adjusted accordingly.

The back
- The waistband line is drawn down by approx. 1 - 2 cm, parallel to the previous one.
- The width of the waistband at the back and the darts must be adjusted accordingly.

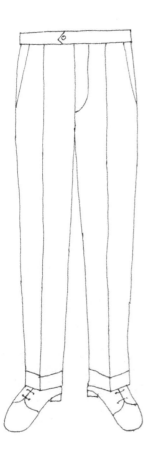

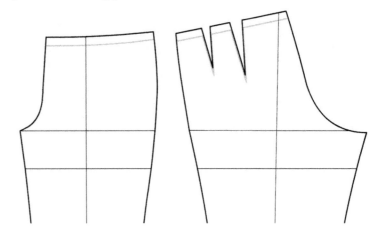

Increasing the rise
- The waistband is too low.
- When sitting, the underpants stick out in the back.

Changes to the pattern
The front
- The waistband line is drawn up by approx. 1 - 2 cm, parallel to the previous one.
- The width of the waistband at the front must be adjusted accordingly.

The back
- The waistband line is drawn up by approx. 1 - 2 cm, parallel to the previous one.
- The width of the waistband at the back and the darts must be adjusted.

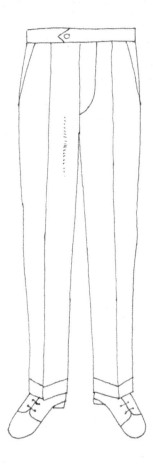

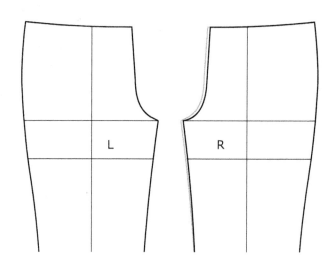

"Package" not considered

- For a good fit, it is important to pay attention to the anatomical characteristics of a man. The side on which the man carries his "package" requires extra width. The other side must be cut narrower at the fly and the inside seam.

Changes to the pattern

- On one side, the fly is cut out by approx. 0.75 cm. The inside seam is adjusted accordingly.

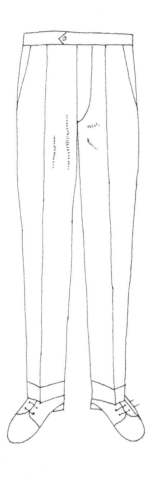

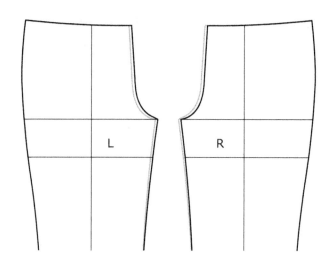

The fly is cut out incorrectly

- In the picture on the left, you can see what happens if the wrong front part is cut narrower.
- Mostly, it is impossible to correct the mistake in the front.
  It takes a lot of effort to hide the problem.
- Cutting out the right side is no problem.
- In order to widen the tight and wrongly cut out fly, the back crotch can be enlarged at the corresponding back part (see p. 48).
- If necessary, the side seam at the hip can also be enlarged at the narrow side (see p. 44).

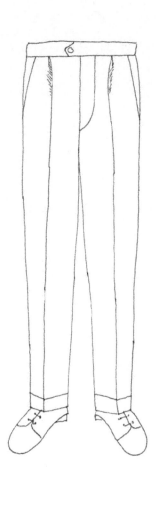

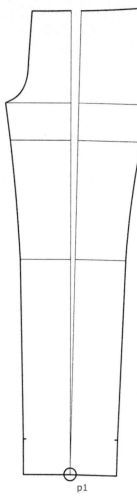

p1

Pleat opens up

(Pictures left)

- The front is too narrow. Therefore, the break does not fall nicely. It stretches and opens up.

Changes to the pattern

- The front pant pattern is cut open at the break line and opened by approx. 1 to 1.5 cm using the pivot point *p1*.
  The width at the 1/2 pants should be at least 1/2 *HIP* + 1/2 depth of pleat + approx. 1 - 1.5 cm fullness).

Too tight at the calf

(Pictures below)

- Especially cyclists have very strong calves. The pants cannot fall around the leg loosely because they get stuck on the calf.

Changes to the pattern

- The back is extended evenly in the calf area by the necessary amount.
- Or the leg is generally marked as wider.

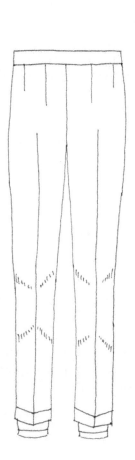

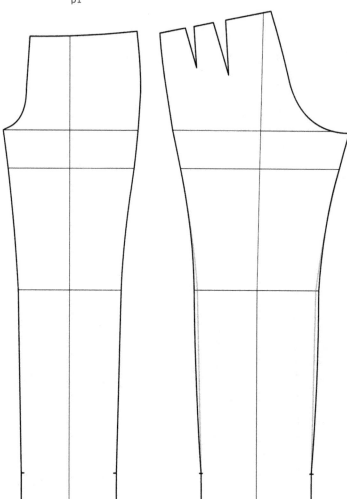

53

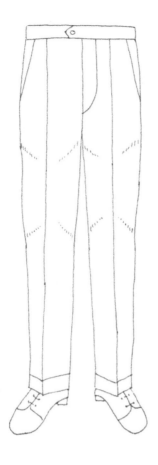
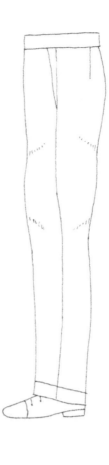

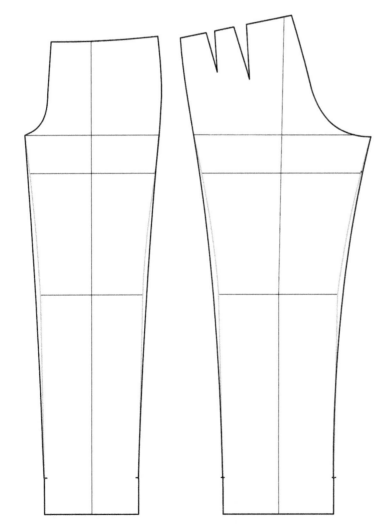

Extending the thigh girth

- The pants are stuck on the thighs and do not fall nicely around the leg.
- For customers with very strong thighs, pants with at least one pleat are recommended.
- If necessary, the break can be drawn deeper or a second pleat or a dart can be added to make the front wider (see also p. 53, pleat opens up).

Changes to the pattern

The front
- The thigh area is evenly extended by approx. 0.5 cm at the side seam and and the inside seam.

The back
- The thigh area is evenly extended by approx. 0.5 cm at the side seam and and the inside seam.

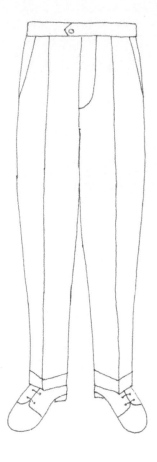
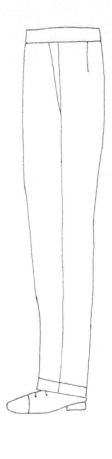

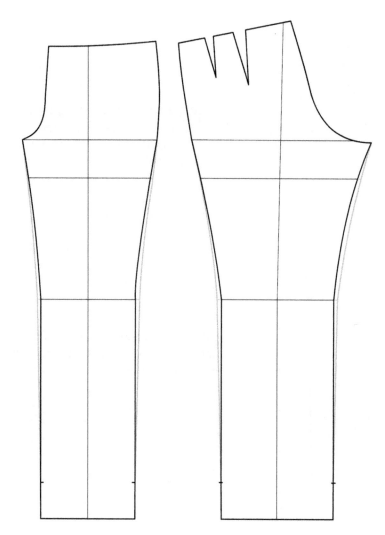

Reducing the thigh girth
- The pants fall very loosely around the thigh.
- The pants are too wide and look "piteous" for the customer.
- It may be possible to omit a pleat, or to keep it very small.

Changes to the pattern
The front
- The thigh area is evenly drawn narrower by approx. 0.5 cm at the side seam and the inside seam.

The back
- The thigh area is evenly drawn narrower at the side seam and at the inside seam.

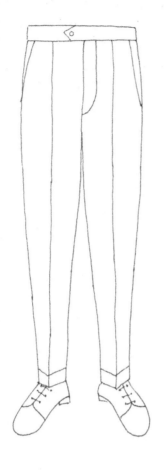
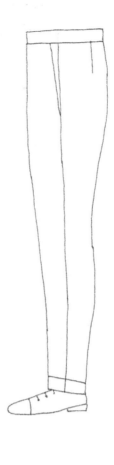

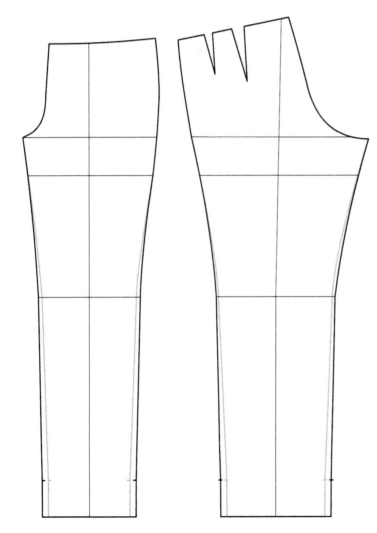

Extending the hem girth
- At the hem, the pants are too
  narrow for the customer, they look
  "peg-top" like.

Changes to the pattern
The front
- At the hem, the side seam and the
  inside seam are evenly drawn wider
  by approx. 1 cm.

The back
- At the hem, the side seam and the
  inside seam are evenly drawn wider
  by approx. 1 cm.

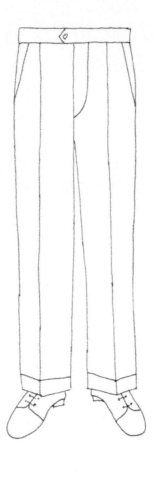

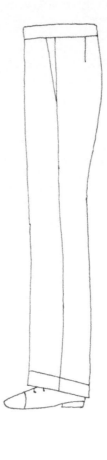

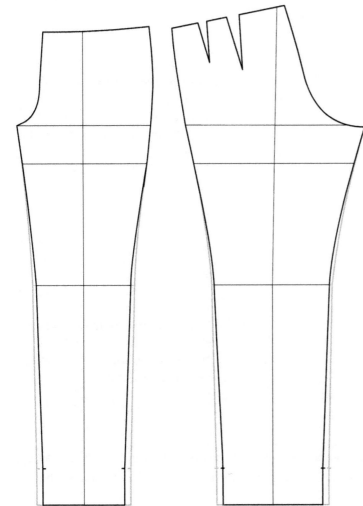

Reducing the hem girth

- The pants fall very loosely on the lower leg.
- For the customer, the pants are too wide and "sloppy".

Changes to the pattern

The front
- At the hem, the side seam and the inside seam are evenly drawn wider by approx. 1 cm.

The back
- At the hem, the side seam and the inside seam are evenly drawn wider by approx. 1 cm.

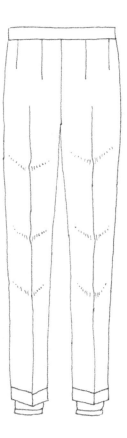

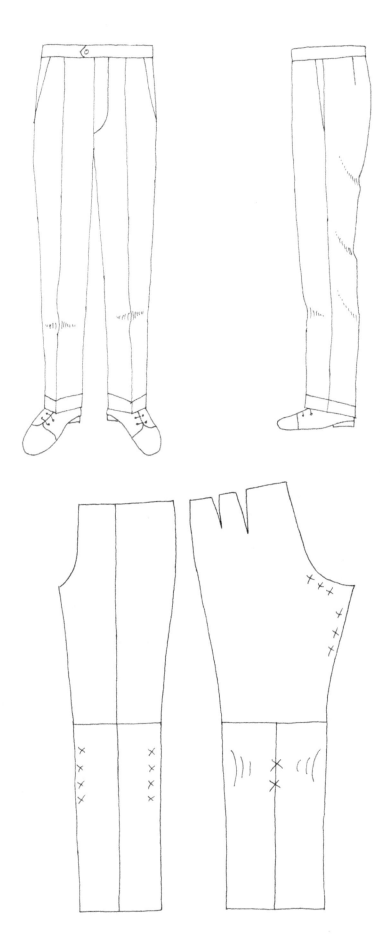

Pressing pants properly
- Without proper pressing (ironing into shape) many avoidable problems arise regarding the fit.

Ironing into shape
The front
- Below the knee point, the side seam and the inside seam at the calf are stretched.
- The break-line can be kept somewhat short.

The back
- Below the knee point, the side seam and inside seam at the calf are kept short.
- The area of the calf can be stretched a little.
- The upper part of the inside seam is stretched.
- In the area of the strong curve, the seat seam is stretched.

Matching up seams correctly
As a result of pressing, the lengths of the side seam and the inside seam of the front and back pants no longer match up. Join the seams at the knee points. After sewing, level the waistband-line and the hem-line by remarking them.

Fitting errors at the vest

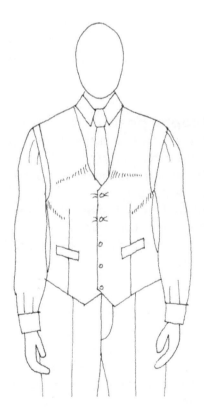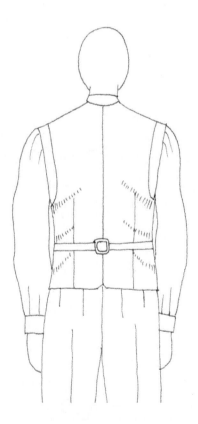

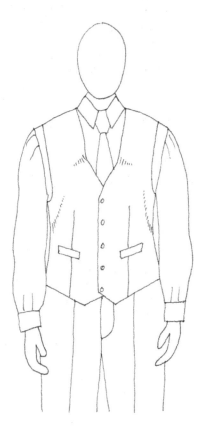

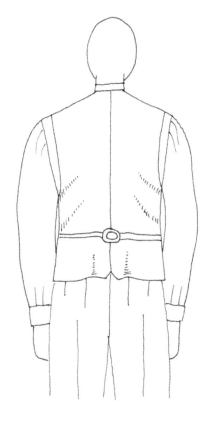

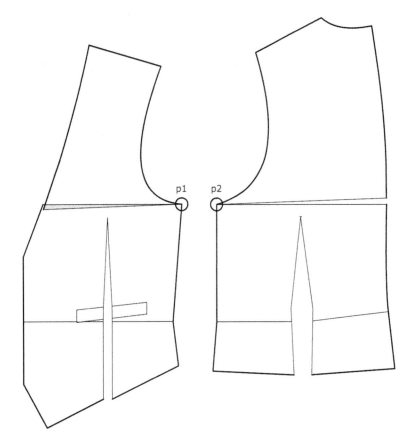

Stooped posture

- There is tension at the upper back in the center back.
- At the back, the hem sticks out in the center back.
- When the vest is open, the lower front edges fall apart.
- Note also the basic types of posture on page 20.

Changes to the pattern

The front
- Cut open the chest-line.
- By using the pivot point *p1*, put together the front edge by approx. 1 cm.

The back
- Cut open the chest-line.
- By using the pivot point *p2*, lay apart the center back by approx. 1 cm.

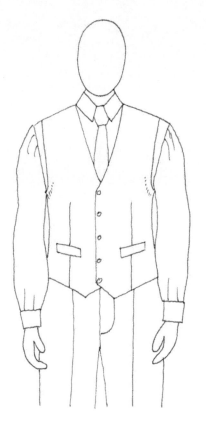 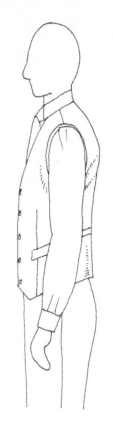 

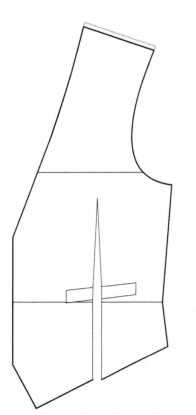 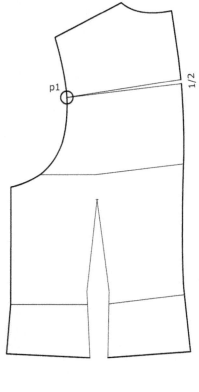

Rounded back

- There are creases forming from the middle of the back to the side seams.
- At the back, the hem sticks out in the center back.
- When the vest is open, the lower front edges fall apart.
- Note also the basic types of posture on page 21.

Changes to the pattern

The back

- At 1/2 depth of scye *DOS*, draw a line parallel to the chest-line and cut open.
- Lay open by approx. 1 cm using the pivot point *p1*.

The front

- Move down the front shoulder seam by approx. 1 cm.

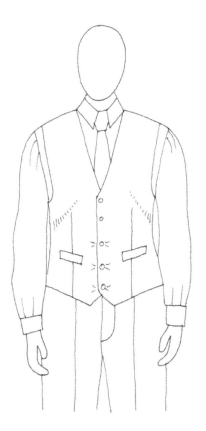
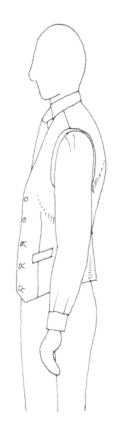

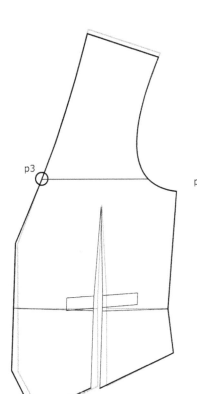
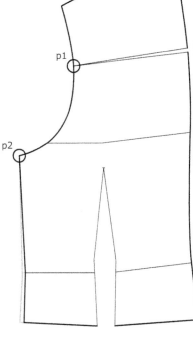

S-shape posture

- There are creases forming from the middle of the back to the side seams.
- There is too much width in the seat area.
- Width is missing on the front parts at the hips and waist.
- Also note the basic types of posture on page 20.

Changes to the pattern

The back

- At 1/2 depth of scye *DOS*, draw a line parallel to the chest-line and cut open.
- Lay open by approx. 1 cm using the pivot point *p1*.
- Draw the side seam narrower by approx. 0.75 cm using the pivot point *p2*.

The front

- Move down the shoulder seam by approx. 1 cm.
- Move the front edge forward by approx. 1.5 cm (double the amount of the alteration at the back side seam) using the pivot point *p3*.
- The grainline corresponds to the new front edge.

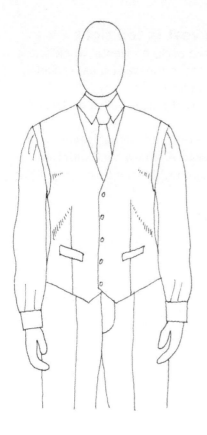

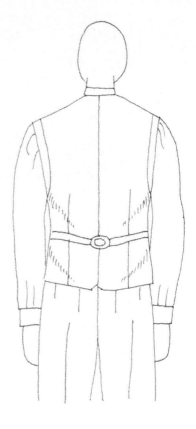

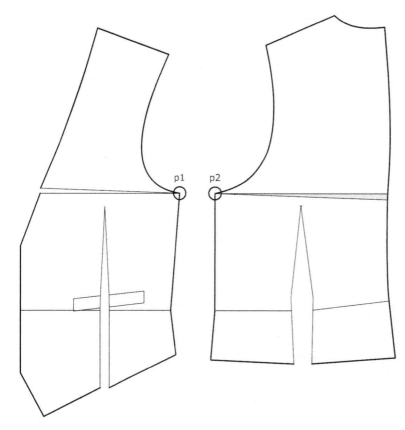

Erect posture
- The vest sticks out slightly at the lower front edge.
- The back stick at the seat.
- When the vest is open, the lower front edges fall apart.
- Note also the basic types of posture on page 20.

Changes to the pattern
The front
- Cut open the chest-line and lay open the front edge by approx. 1 cm using the pivot point *p1*.

The back
- Cut open the chest-line and put together the center back by approx. 1 cm using the pivot point *p2*.

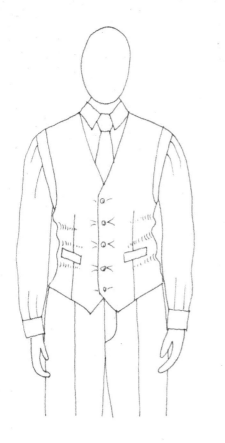 

The vest is too tight

- At the back, horizontal wrinkles are formed in the waist area, radiating to the front.
- The front part is pulled backward.

- If there is not enough seam allowance, a new back with the required width can be cut.

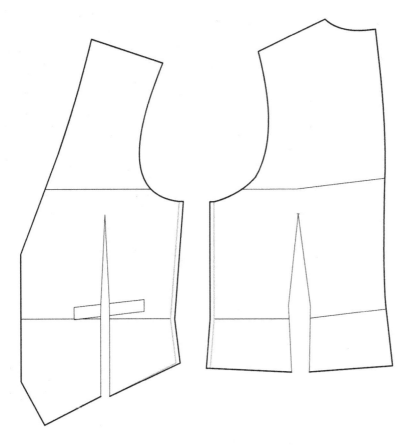

Changes to the pattern

The front
- The entire side seam is extended by the desired amount.

The back
- The entire side seam is extended by the desired amount.

Note

If this is the first fitting, the missing width should be divided equally between the center front, side seams, and center back.

 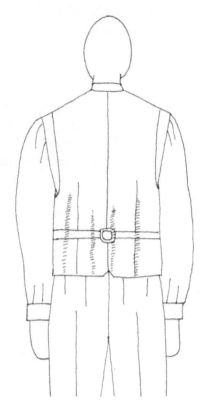

The vest is too loose
- The vest appears too wide overall.
- The front and back fit the customer loosely and shapelessly.

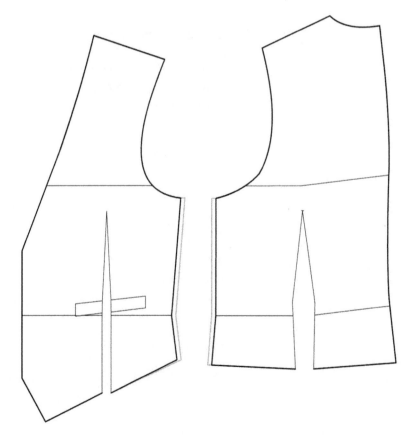

Changes to the pattern
The front
- The entire side seam is drawn narrower by the desired amount.

The back
- The entire side seam is drawn narrower by the desired amount.

Note
If this is the first fitting, the width should be taken in equally at the center front, side seam, and center back.

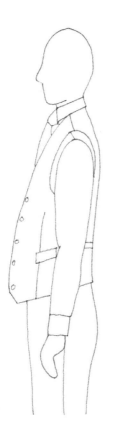

The lower front edge sticks out

- The front edge sticks out from the waist towards the front.
- Possibly, a slightly pronounced belly was not considered.
- Possibly it is a slight S-shape posture, as well.

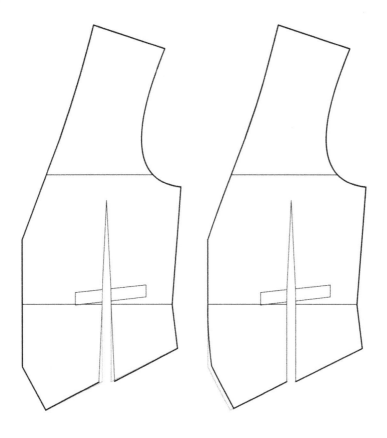

Changes to the pattern

Option 1

- On the front, the chest dart is enlarged (drawn deeper) from the waist down.

Option 2

- The front edge can be drawn narrower from the waist down.

Note

Both options can also be combined with each other.

For the next vest, the pattern should be altered for a belly.

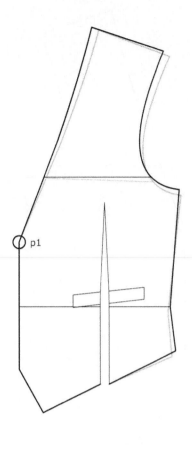

The edges overlap too much at the top

- The front edges are not straight and overlap each other a lot in the chest area.
- The shoulder section is twisted.

Changes to the pattern

- Using the pivot point *p1*, the upper and back parts of the front are turned forward by approx. 1 cm.
- The front edge and the dart remain unaffected.

Note

The side seam may also have to be narrowed after this alteration.

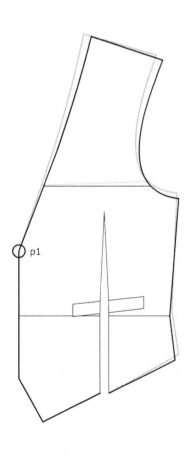

The edges overlap too much at the bottom

- The front edges are not straight and overlap each other a lot in the waist area.
- The shoulder section is twisted.

Changes to the pattern

- Using the pivot point *p1*, the upper and back parts of the front are turned backward by approx. 1 cm.
- The front edge and the dart remain unaffected.

Note

The side seam may also have to be narrowed after this alteration.

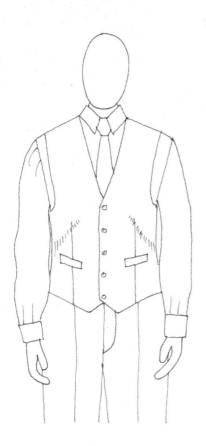

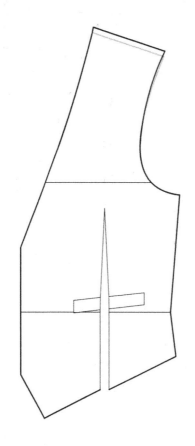

The front part is too short

- Diagonal folds are formed below the armhole, pulling forward towards the chest.

Changes to the pattern

- At the front, the shoulder seam is moved upwards by the desired amount.
- The shape of the neckline and armhole may have to be compensated.

Strong chest

- The front opening sticks out at the neckline.
- In the case of a very strong chest, the front may also be too short.
- Not to be confused with a wrong shoulder position (see p. 69) or bad pressing (see p. 76).

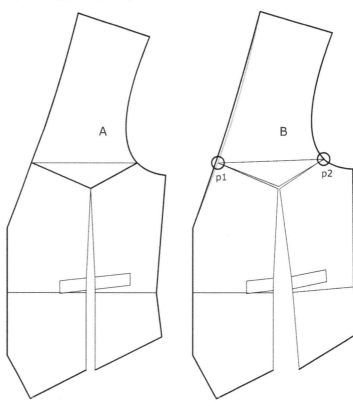

Changes to the pattern:

A:
- From the tip of the dart to the chestline draw up diagonally and cut open.

B:
- At the tip of the dart, the two lower parts are turned outwards by approx. 0.5 cm each using the pivot points *p1* and *p2*.

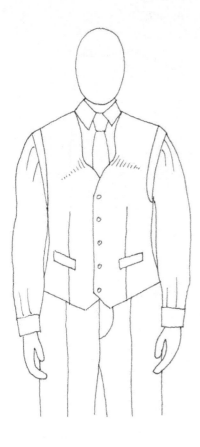

The front opening sticks out

- The front opening has too much length. Thus, a fold is formed.
- Not to be confused with bad or false pressing (see p. 76).

Changes to the pattern

- The shoulder section is moved to the left using the pivot point *p1*.
- The course of the lines of the front opening and the armhole must be adjusted afterward.

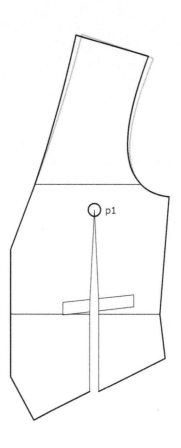

The armhole sticks out

- The armhole has too much length. Thus, a fold is formed.
- Not to be confused with bad pressing (see p. 76).

Changes to the pattern

- The shoulder section is moved to the right using the pivot point p1.
- The course of the lines of the front opening and the armhole must be adjusted afterward.

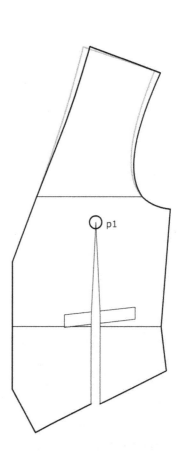

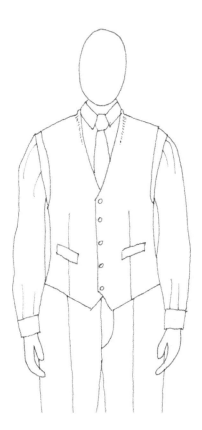

The neckline is too close to the neck

- The neckline pushes against the neck, causing a vertical fold.

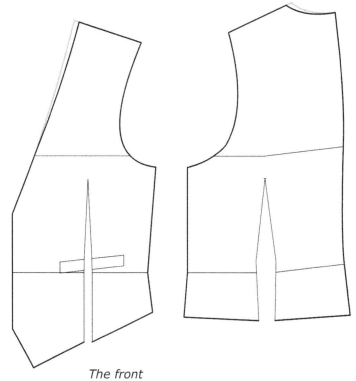

Changes to the pattern

The back

- The neckline is extended by the desired measurement at the shoulder seam.

The front

- The front neckline is moved by the same amount.
- This makes the shoulder seam narrower.
- The back shoulder seam must be approx. 0.5 - 0.75 cm longer than the front shoulder seam (fullness during tailoring).

The neckline is too far from the neck

- The neckline is far from the collar.
- Between shirt collar and vest neckline is a significant distance.

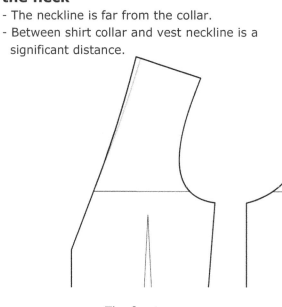

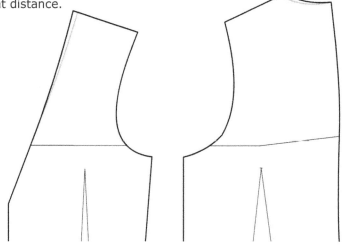

The front

- The front neckline is widened by the same amount.
- This makes the shoulder seam wider.
- The back shoulder seam must be approx. 0.5 - 0.75 cm longer than the front shoulder seam (fullness during construction).

Changes to the pattern

The back

- The neckline is narrowed at the shoulder seam by the desired amount.

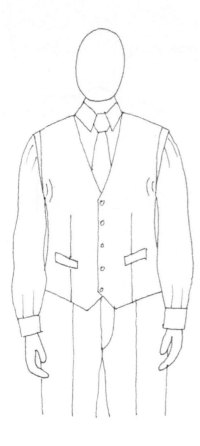

The front armhole is bulging

- The front piece is pushing into the armhole, so the front is bulging.
- The customer feels like the armhole is too tight.

Changes to the pattern

- At the front, the armhole is cut out a little forward.

Note

It is important to find out whether the armhole is tight in the front or pushing up under the arm. If the last one is the case, the armhole is too high and has to be cut out (see p. 74).

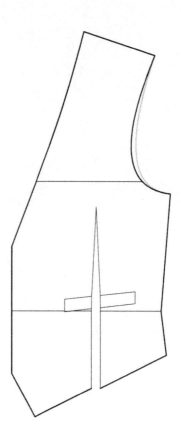

The armhole is cut out too far

- At the armhole, a lot of the shirt's front is visible.
- The armhole is cut out very far to the front.
- The customer finds the armhole very comfortable, but it looks strange.

Changes to the pattern

- If this is the first fitting and you have seam allowances, the armhole at the front may be marked less pronounced.
- Unfortunately, it is impossible to make any changes to a finished vest.

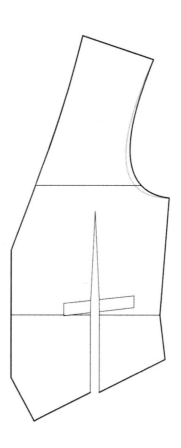

Square shoulders
- The armhole is too short in the upper area.
  This creates length at the neckline.

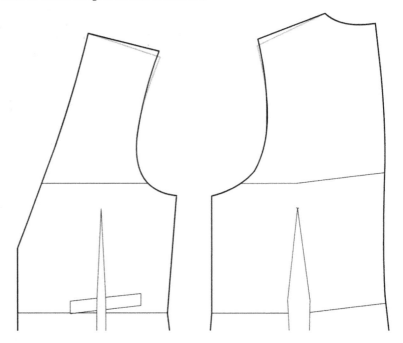

Changes to the pattern
- The shoulder seams of the front and back pieces
  are drawn upwards by the desired amount at
  the armhole.

Sloping shoulders
- The armhole is sagging in the upper area.
- The resulting length can easily be pinned.

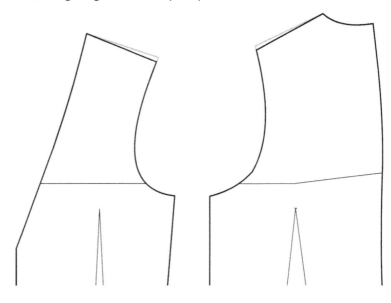

Changes to the pattern
- The shoulder seams of the front and back pieces
  are drawn downwards by the desired amount at
  the armhole.

Shoulders are too wide

- The front piece is much too wide at the shoulders, the armhole extends to the shirt sleeve seam or beyond.

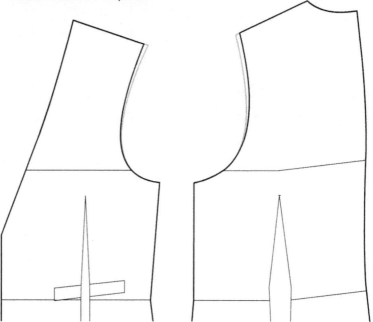

Changes to the pattern

- At the shoulders, the armhole at the front and back is drawn narrower by the desired amount.

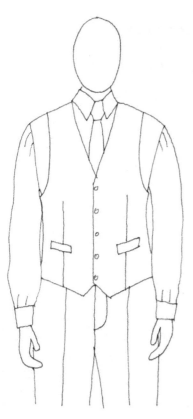

Shoulders are too narrow

- The front part is much too narrow at the shoulders, so the shoulders appear very wide.

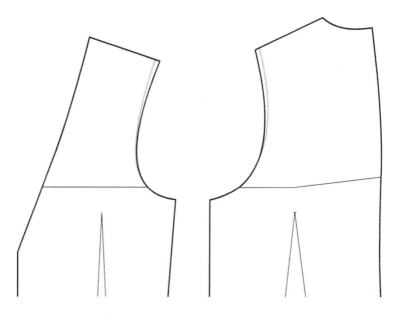

Changes to the pattern

- At the shoulders, the armhole at the front and back is drawn wider by the desired amount.

The armhole is too high

- The armhole pushes up into the customer's armpit from below. The fabric is bulging under the arm.

Changes to the pattern
The front
- The armhole is drawn lower by the desired amount.

The back
- The armhole is drawn lower by the desired amount.

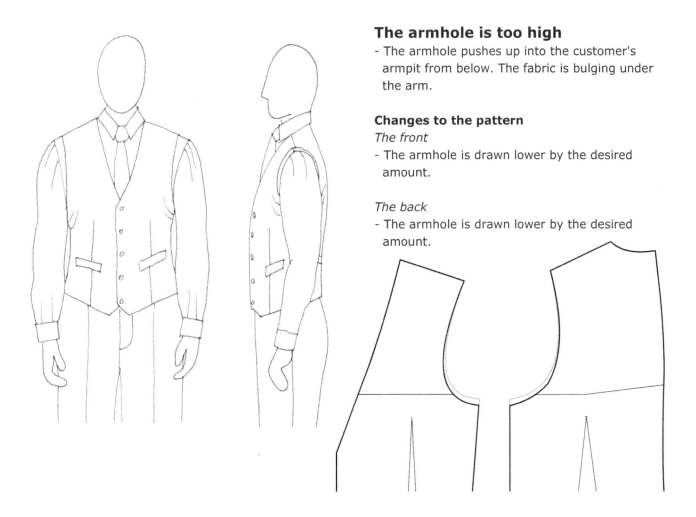

The armhole is too low

- The armhole does not end at the sleeve seam of the shirt. The armhole is much too low.

Changes to the pattern
The front
- The armhole is drawn higher by the desired amount.

The back
- The armhole is drawn higher by the desired amount.

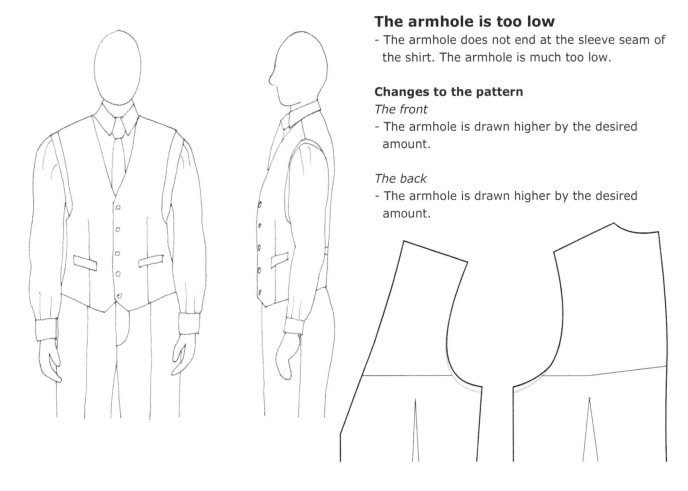

The back is too long

- Creases form from the side seam toward the center back.
- The back lies on the seat and thus bulges in the waist area.

Changes to the pattern

- A line is drawn at half the depth of scye *DOS* parallel to the chest-line and cut open.
- The two resulting pieces are now joined together evenly.

Note

For a vest to feel comfortable, the back needs a certain length. It is perfect if you feel the back should be shorter by about 1 - 1.5 cm. In this case, please ignore any changes.

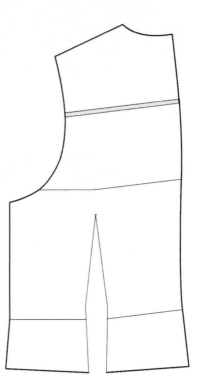

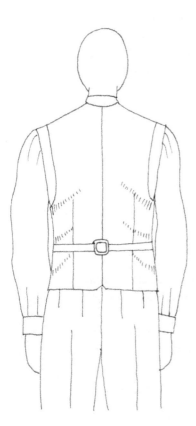

The back is too short

- Creases form from the side seam toward the center back.
- In the center back, the back part pulls upwards.

Changes to the pattern

- A line is drawn at half the depth of scye *DOS* parallel to the chest-line and cut open.
- The two resulting pieces are now pulled apart evenly.

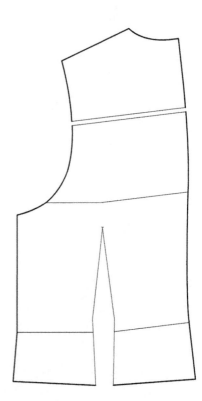

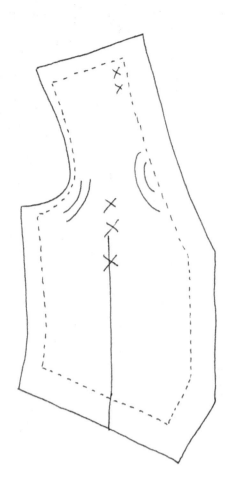

Pressing a vest properly

Both front parts should be placed with the right side facing each other and ironed in shape evenly.

- The neck opening is kept short.
- The front armhole is kept short at the strongest part of the curve.
- The upper part at the neck opening is slightly stretched for the shoulder.
- The chest area is slightly stretched.

Note

- In the case of stripes or checks, the fabric pattern must be even and not warped.
- During the entire process, care should be taken to ensure that the armhole and the neck opening do not stretch again.

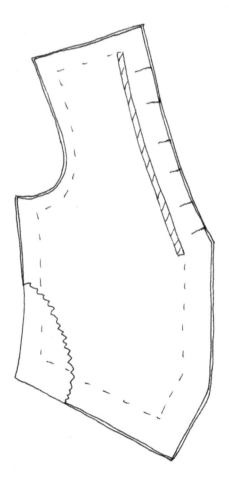

Stabilizing the neck opening

To prevent the vest neck opening from expanding, it is held in place using a tape made of cotton or lining material.

- Directly behind the line of the neck opening, the tape is attached.
- Depending on the wearer's chest's strength, it should be kept short, more or less.
- Usually, it is sufficient to pin on the tape shorter by approx. 1 cm.
- Of course, a fusible tape can also be used.

Stabilizing the front armhole

- Before sewing the lining to the armhole, the armhole of the vest should be kept short once again.
- Later, the armhole is protected from stretching by the lining.

ting errors at the jacket

erect posture
vertical position
means that the
ity by nature.
change the

teration for the
ne from the
quare left and
er part of the
he alteration is
ant effect on firm

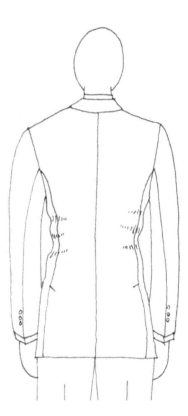

alteration for the
e from the sleeve-
left and right.
rt of the sleeve

Stooped posture

Normal posture

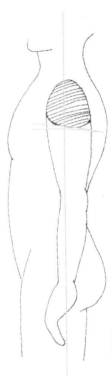

Erect posture

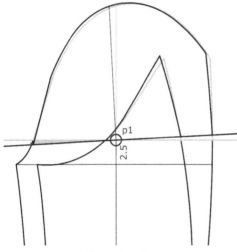

Stooped posture

The sleeve before cutting

Adjusting the sleeve for a stooped o
The posture also affects the sleeve. The
of the arms determines the posture. This
freely hanging arm always yields to grav
But diseases or strong muscles can also
sleeve pitch.

Stooped posture
The upper pattern drawing shows the a
stooped posture. At the sleeve-center-l
sleeve-head-line mark up 2.5 cm and s
right. Using the pivot point *p1*, the upp
sleeve head is tilted slightly forward. T
only minimally visible but has a signific
fabrics.

Erect posture
The lower pattern drawing shows the
erect posture. At the sleeve-center-lir
head-line mark up 2.5 cm and square
Using the pivot point *p1*, the upper pa
head is tilted slightly backward.

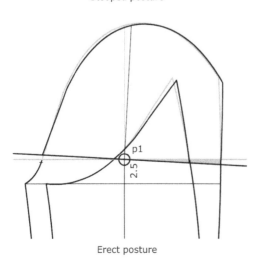

Erect posture

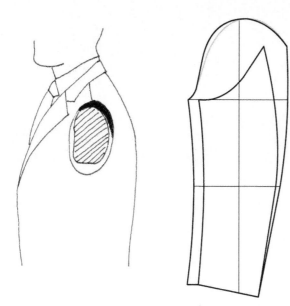

Rounded shoulders

In the case of rounded shoulders, the shoulder joint is moved forward, pushing the shoulder blade outward and making the back appear strongly curved.

A shoulder pad in the usual place, in the middle, would make the shoulder bone even more prominent and become very uncomfortable. But if the shoulder pad is placed backward, the shoulder is given more freedom for movement. This way, the low placed padding compensates a little for the strong shoulder blades.

This gives the armhole a natural, even shape. In the pattern, the sleeve head must be redrawn accordingly and gets a little more width at the front. In the back area, it becomes a little flatter (see also stooped posture on p. 78).

Differences in the shoulder position

The small image shows the difference between the two shoulder positions (the dotted line represents the position of the retracted shoulder).

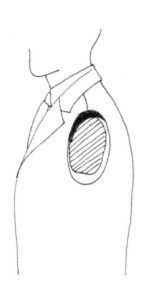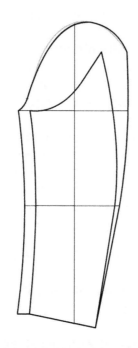

Retracted shoulders

The opposite is true for retracted shoulders. The shoulder pad is moved forward, i.e., it sits partly in front of the shoulder bone. If the padding is not placed forward, the fullness at the back cannot roll to the armhole in the correct manner.

This is a common mistake, which usually has its cause here. In the pattern, the sleeve head must be redrawn accordingly and is flattened slightly at the front (see also erect posture on p. 78).

Observe when taking measurements

Especially with rounded shoulders, it is challenging and almost impossible to make changes later on. Therefore, it is necessary to consider the shoulder shape when taking measurements and include this in the pattern drawing. Softer fabrics can be very forgiving. But fabrics that are firmer or have a plaid pattern must be cut correctly from the start.

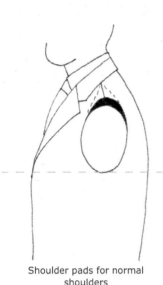

Shoulder pads for normal
shoulders

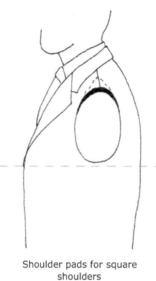

Shoulder pads for square
shoulders

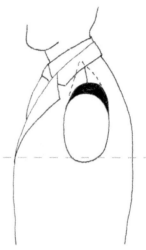

Shoulder pads for slope
shoulders

Shoulder pads

The shoulder pads significantly influence the shoulder shape and, thus, the fashionable silhouette of the jacket.

Uneven shoulders can be compensated. Heavily sloping shoulders are straightened a little. However, shoulder pads that are too high can become very uncomfortable when moving. In current fashion trends, relatively thin shoulder pads are preferred.

It is best to make the shoulder pads individually for each customer. But you can also use ready-made cushions and adjust them in the desired shape. Under no circumstances you should use unchanged shoulder pads out of laziness.

The placement of the padding is also critical, as the previous pages showed. Therefore, it is important to mark the position after the fittings so that the pads can be secured in the same place again.

Changes to the sleeve pattern

On the right, you can see the most common types of sleeve adjustments. Of course, you can incorporate the changes right away when drawing the pattern. However, if you do not want to set up a sleeve pattern every time and use templates in the basic sizes, you can easily modify them according to the instructions provided.

The strong upper arm
The upper and undersleeves are cut open at the sleeve-center-line. At the back, the sleeve-head-line is opened. Use the pivot point *p1* to give the upper arm the necessary width. The back sleeve head is opened to the same amount using the pivot point *p2*. Now the back-sleeve-seam must be adjusted.

Widening the sleeve at the top
If the sleeve is too short inside the armhole, it can be widened using the pivot point *p1*. The affected seams must be adjusted.

Tightening the sleeve at the top
If the sleeve is too wide inside the armscye, it can be narrowed using the pivot point *p1*. The affected seams must be adjusted.

Widening or lengthening the entire sleeve
The sleeve-center-line and the elbow-line are cut open. Then the pieces can be moved parallel to each other. This is especially useful when a standard sleeve is used. The affected seams must be adjusted.

Narrowing or shortening the entire sleeve
The procedure is the same as for widening or lengthening, but in the opposite direction (see above).

Heavily angled sleeve
The upper and lower sleeves are cut open at the elbow-line. Using the pivot point *p1*, the lower part of the sleeve is turned forward to the required angle.

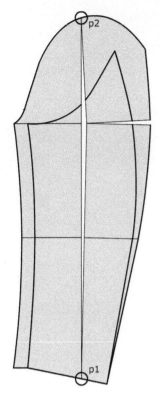

The strong upper arm

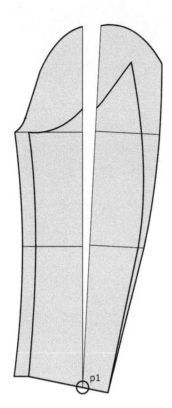

Widening the sleeve at the top

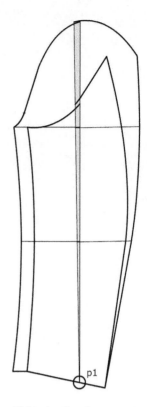

Tightening the sleeve
at the top

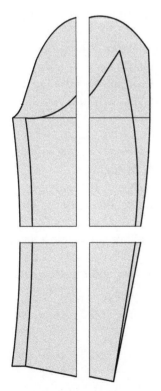

Widening or lengthening the
entire sleeve

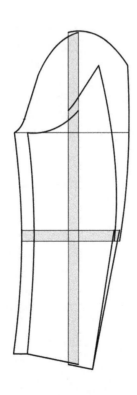

Narrowing or shortening the
entire sleeve

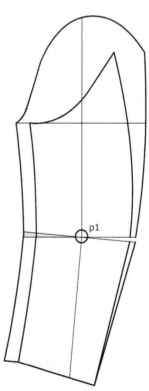

Heavily angled sleeve

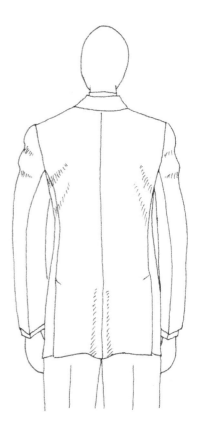

Stooped posture

This posture positions its whole upper body towards the front. In contrast to the "rounded back", where the spine is round at the level of the shoulder blades, here, the whole back is round up to the waist. The jacket is too short across the entire back. In the stooped position, the arms often go forward. The shoulders can be pushed forward.

Diagnosis

- From the side, the jacket is much longer at the front than at the back.
- The upper back is too tight in the center back.
- The length at the center back sticks out.
- The back slit or the side slits fall together too much
- When the jacket is open, the front edges fall apart at the bottom.

Often in combination with

- Rounded back
- High sleeve pitch

Rarely in combination with

- Strong chest
- Low sleeve pitch
- Pleat at the neck

Changes to the pattern

- Mark the pivot point at the side piece, at the center of the chest-line. Then cut open the pattern.
- Rotate forward the front piece by approx. 1 - 2 cm (depending on the characteristics of the posture) using the pivot point *p1*.
  This will cause the back piece to open up by the same amount and gain length.
- The back seam, the lapel break, and the lapel edge, as well as the side seams, must be adjusted accordingly.

To be considered during tailoring

- Since the chest is often flat with this posture, the chest area is pressed (ironed in shape) only a little.
- Also, do not keep the lapel break too short when pressing (see p. 126).
- The sleeve is inserted too low and must be rotated a little forward (see p. 112).

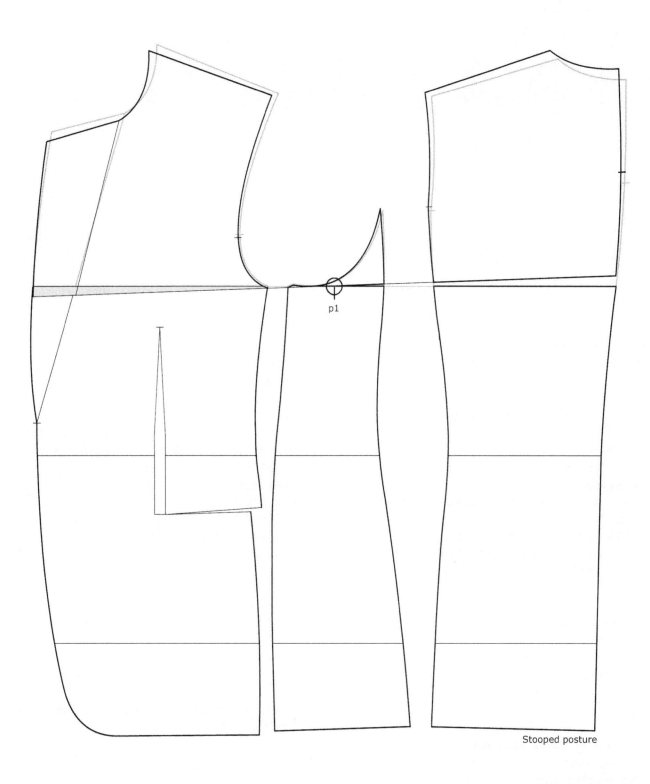

p1

Stooped posture

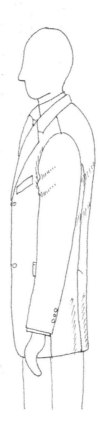
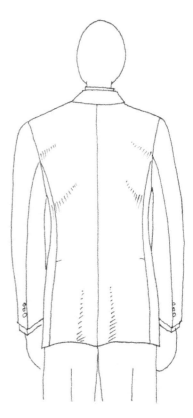

Rounded back

In the area of the shoulder blades, the spine is rounded. The jacket is too short at the upper part of the back. In contrast to the S-shape, this shape is otherwise straight, or the upper body is tilted forward.

Diagnosis

- Folds are forming from the center back to the side seams.
- The length at the center back sticks out.
- The collar has a tendency not to stay at the neck.
- The lower front edges may fall apart.

Often in combination with

- Stooped posture
- Less pronounced chest
- Sloping shoulders
- Rounded shoulders

Rarely in combination with

- Strong chest
- Square shoulders
- Low sleeve pitch

Changes to the pattern

- Draw a line on the back at 1/2 depth of scye *DOS* parallel to the chest-line and extend it to the front part.
- Rotate open the back by approx. 1 cm using the pivot point *p1*, according to the intensity of the rounded back.
- Rotate together the front by approx. 1 cm using the pivot point *p2*.
- The center back seam, the armhole, the lapel break, and the lapel edge must be adjusted accordingly.

To be considered during tailoring

- Since the chest is often flat with this posture, the chest area is pressed (ironed in shape) just slightly.
- Also, do not keep the lapel break too short when pressing (see p. 126).
- The sleeve is inserted too low and must be rotated a little forward (see p. 112).

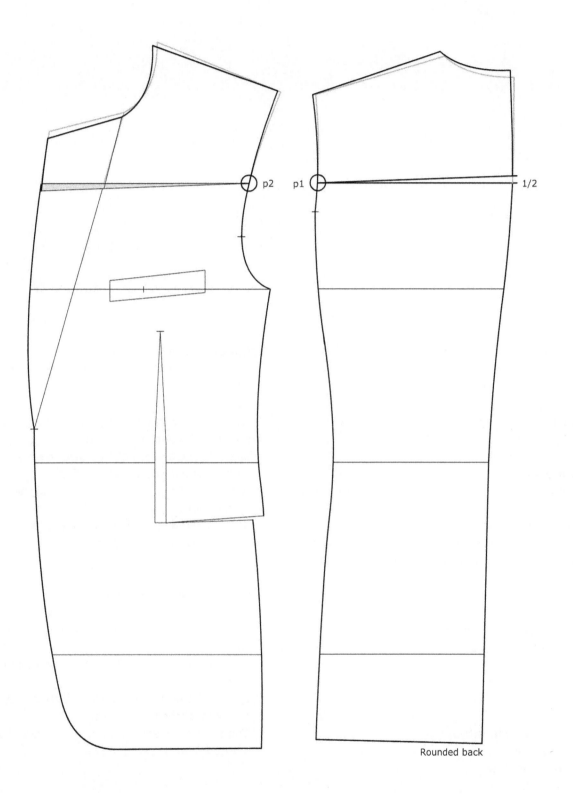

p2   p1   1/2

Rounded back

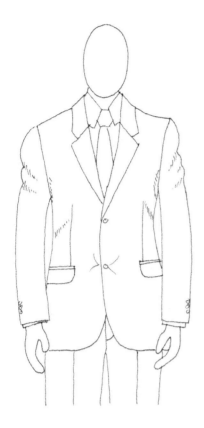

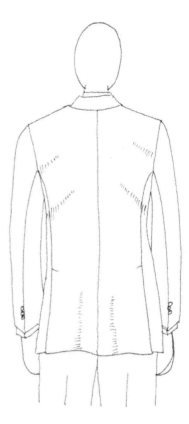

S-shape posture

This shape also has a rounded back, but rather a bent (collapsed) posture. In addition, the belly and hips are pushed forward. With a rounded back, the back length is too short; the back pulls the jacket away from the neck.

Diagnosis

- Folds are forming from the center back to the side seams.
- There is too much width in the seat area.
- The collar has a tendency not to stay at the neck.
- There is missing width on the front parts at the hip and waist level.

Often in combination with

- Less pronounced chest
- Sloping shoulders
- Rounded shoulders

Rarely in combination with

- Strong chest
- Square shoulders
- Fold at the neck

Changes to the pattern

- At the upper back and the upper front, the same alterations are performed as for the rounded back (see p. 84).
- Draw the side seam at the lower part of the back narrower by approx. 0.5 cm.
- Draw the side seam at the lower part of the side piece narrower by approx. 0.5 cm.
- Rotate the front piece forward using the pivot point p3 by approx. one and a half times the total amount removed at the side seam (approx 1.5 cm). Adjust all affected lines accordingly.

To be considered during tailoring

- Since the chest is often flat with this posture, the chest area is pressed (ironed in shape) only a little.
- Also, do not keep the lapel break too short when pressing (see p. 126).
- Due to the prominent belly, the chest dart can sometimes be omitted.
- The sleeve is inserted too low and must be rotated a little forward (see p. 112).

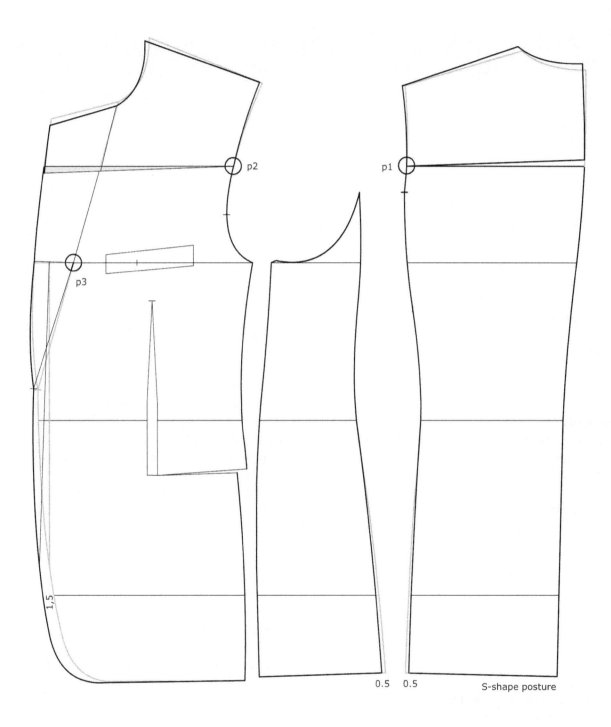

p2

p1

p3

1,5

0.5   0.5

S-shape posture

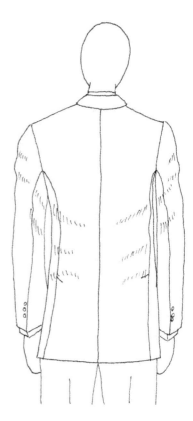

Erect posture

Here the sleeve pitch is often too high.
The shoulders are retracted, and the shoulder blades push towards each other.

Diagnosis
- From the side, the jacket is shorter at the front than at the back.
- The lower back lies on the seat.
- The back slit or the side slits opens up.
- When the jacket is open, the lower front edges overlap each other.

Often in combination with
- Strong chest
- Pointed belly
- Fold at the neck
- Low sleeve pitch

Rarely in combination with
- Less pronounced chest
- High sleeve pitch

Changes to the pattern
- Mark the pivot point at the center of the chest-line. Then cut open the pattern.
- Rotate together the back by approx. 0.5 - 1 cm (depending on the characteristics of the posture) using the pivot point *p1*.
- The front is rotated open by approx. 1 - 2 cm (approx. twice as much as at the back) using the pivot point *p1*.
- The back seam, the lapel break, and the lapel edge as well as the side seams must be adjusted accordingly.

To be considered during tailoring
- Since the chest is often strong with this posture, the chest area has to be pressed (ironed into shape) more (see p. 126).
- Also, keep the lapel break slightly short.
- The sleeve is inserted too high and must be rotated a little backward (see p. 112).

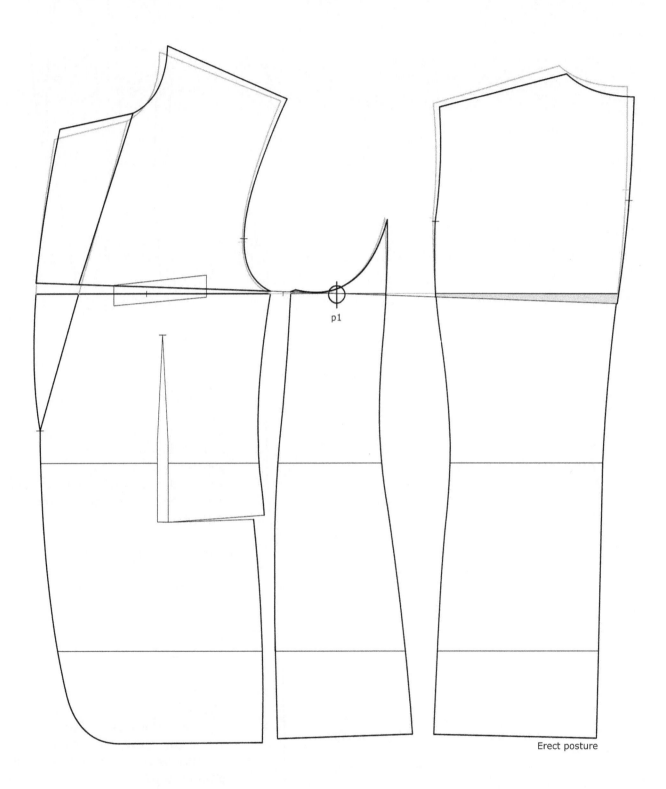

p1

Erect posture

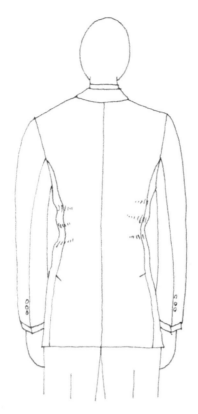
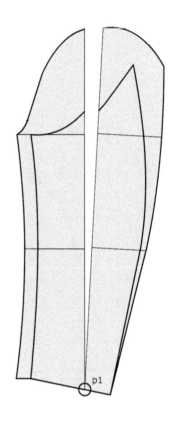

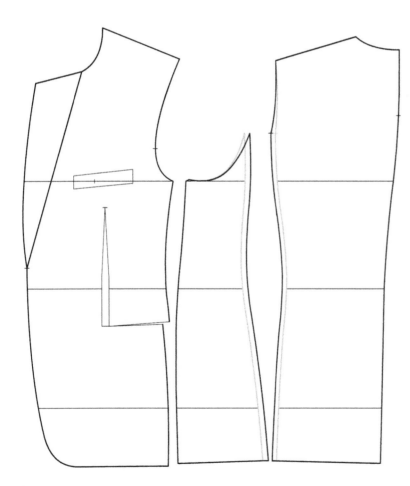

The jacket is too tight

- At the back, horizontal wrinkles are formed in the waist area, causing folds at the front. The front part is pulled backward.
- As with the width-of-scye that is too narrow, the armhole presses the customer's arm at the front.

Changes to the pattern

The jacket

- At the side piece, the entire side seam is extended by the desired measurement.
- At the back, the side seam is extended by the same measurement.

The sleeve

- The sleeve is now too small for the armhole and is therefore enlarged.
- The sleeve center line is cut open and the sleeve is extended using the pivot point *p1*.
- The affected seams at the sleeve head and at the armhole seam of the under sleeve must be compensated (see also p. 80).

Note

If this is the first fitting, the missing width should be divided equally between the center front, side seam, and center back.

 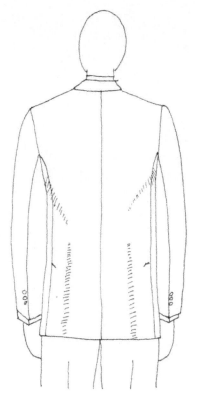 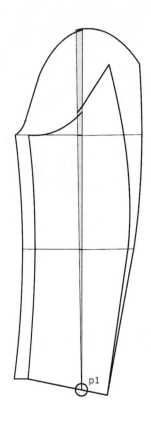

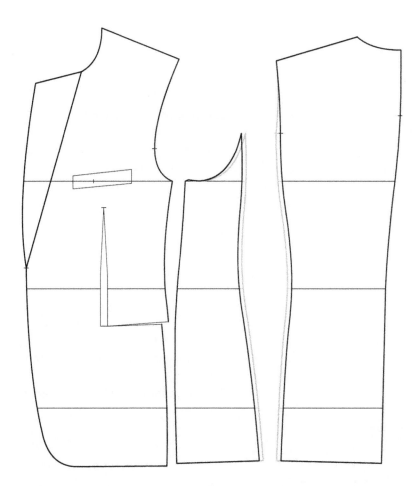

The jacket is too loose
- The jacket appears too wide overall.
- Especially the front part is "flapping" around.

Changes to the pattern
The jacket
- At the side piece, the entire side seam is narrowed by the desired amount.
- At the back, the side seam is narrowed by the same amount.

The sleeve
- The sleeve is too wide now for the armhole and therefore is made narrower.
- The sleeve center line is cut open, and the sleeve is put together using the pivot point *p1*.
- The affected seams at the sleeve head and the armhole seam of the under sleeve must be adjusted (see also p. 80).

Note
If this is the first fitting, the width should be divided equally between the center front, side seam, and center back.

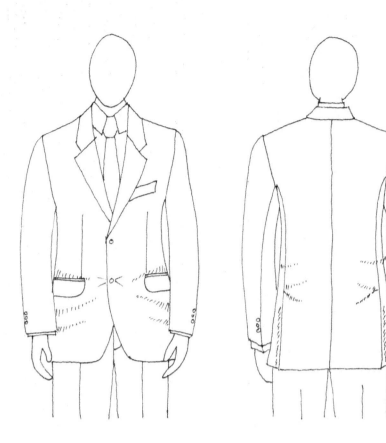

The seat is too tight

- On the back, horizontal wrinkles are formed in the hip area, which causes the front part to form folds.
  The front is pulled backward.
- When the lower button is closed, the jacket tightens around the hips.
- When the button is open, the edges fall apart.

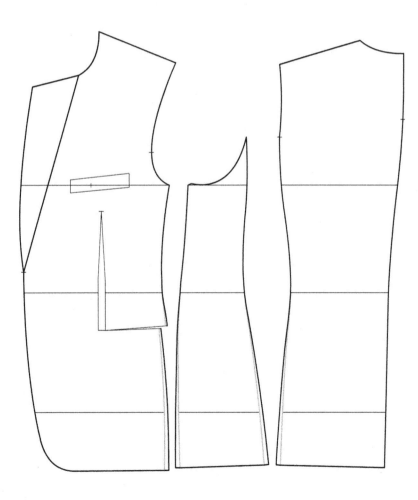

Changes to the pattern

The side part
- On the side part, the side seam at the hip curve is extended by the desired measurement.

The back
- On the back, the side seam at the hip curve is extended by the same measurement.

The seam on the side part
- In the case of a strong hip, it is advisable to extend the side part seam as well (at the front and the side part).
- This is usually the strongest part of the hip.

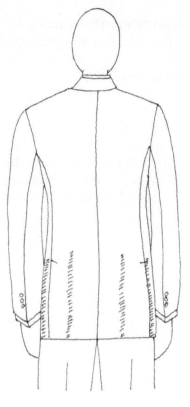

The seat is too loose
- Vertical folds form on the back in the hip area.
- The excess material is visible, and the fabric flaps in this area.
- Vertical folds are also forming in the hip area on the front.
- When the button is open, the edges fall toward each other.

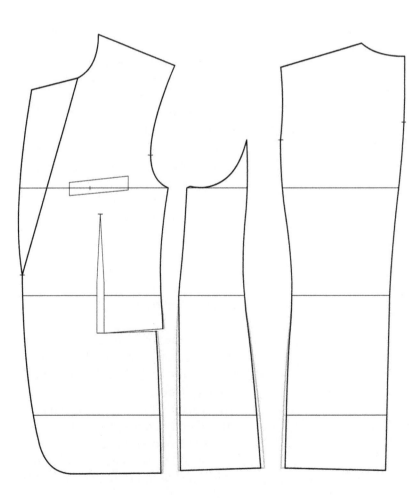

Changes to the pattern
The side part
- On the side part, the side seam on the hip arch is drawn narrower by the desired amount.

The back
- At the back, the side seam at the hip curve is narrowed by the same amount.

The seam on the side part
- If the hip is very flat, it is advisable to also narrow the side part seam (at the front and at the side part).

Rounded shoulders
- The shoulders are pushed forward.

Diagnosis
- At the front below the collar, a fold is formed, which can extend to the armhole.
- The customer feels an unpleasant pressure at the front of the shoulder.
- When the jacket is open, the front edges can fall apart.
- Attention, not to be confused with the fold at the neck (only visible on the back) or square shoulders.

Often in combination with
- Less pronounced chest
- S-shape posture
- Rounded back

Rarely in combination with
- Sloping shoulder

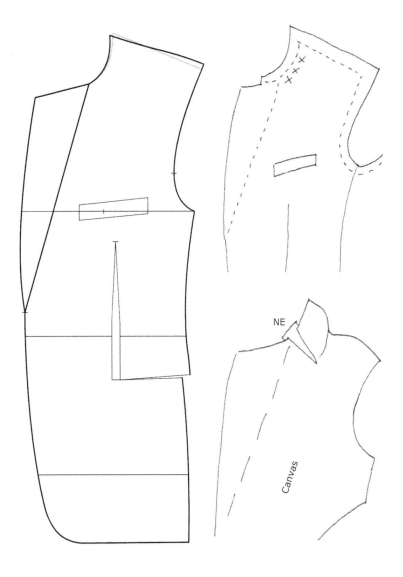

Changes to the pattern
- First, try to solve this problem by better tailoring. If it is not sufficient to relocate the shoulder pads or to press the shoulder (ironing into a form), the shoulder seam at the armhole is corrected upward by approx. 0.5 - 1 cm (depending on intensity, see the pattern on the far left).
- At the neckline, the shoulder seam is lowered by approx. 0.5 cm, at the front, approx. 0.5 cm will be added (due to the intense pressing, these areas return to their previous position).

To be considered during tailoring
- The shoulder pads must be repositioned to the back (see also page 79).
  Besides, the front piece (drawing on the upper left) must be stretched (ironed into shape) at the neckline (at the crosses).
- The canvas (drawing on the left) should be altered accordingly.
- It may be necessary to open the canvas at the neckline (NE) a little more to give the shoulder more room in the front.

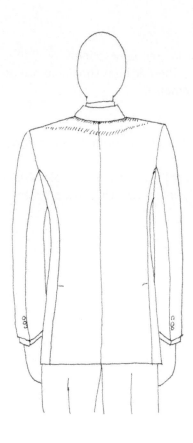

Square shoulders

- Square shoulders can occur in any body shape.
- Special attention must be paid to whether both shoulders are at the same angle or there is an asymmetry.

Diagnosis

- On the back, below the collar, a large horizontal fold is formed. This may also be seen on the front part.
- The jacket collar does not stay at the neck.
- When the jacket is open, the front edges fall apart at the hem.
- Attention, not to be confused with the fold at the neck or rounded shoulders.

Often in combination with

- Erect posture

Rarely in combination with

- S-shape posture
- Rounded back
- Asymmetrically sloping shoulders

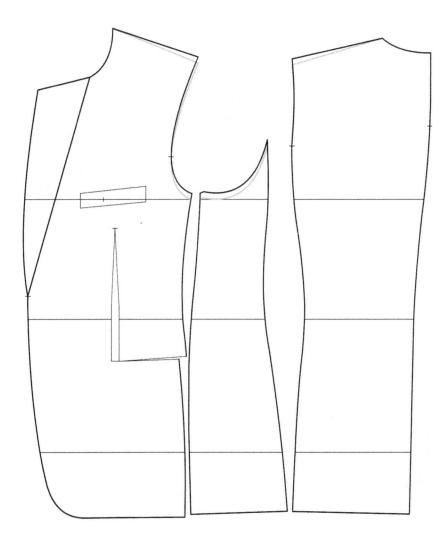

Changes to the pattern

- The shoulder seams at the armhole and the depth-of-scye *DOS* are corrected upward, depending on the intensity of the square shoulder.
- Nothing changes at the neck.

For more information on shoulder angle and padding thickness, see page 80.

To be considered during tailoring

- If the shoulders are asymmetrical, they can be compensated with different shoulder pads. Either a thinner pad is used for the square shoulder or a thicker pad for the normal shoulder.

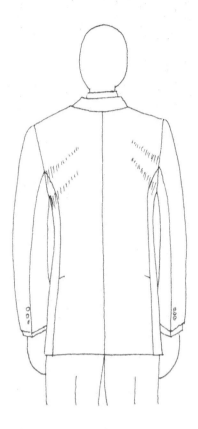

Sloping shoulders
- Sloping or low shoulders can occur in any body shape.
- Special attention should be paid to whether both shoulders are at the same angle or there is an asymmetry.

Diagnosis
- Starting at the neck point, diagonal folds are formed on the back towards the lower armhole area.
- In the front, the chest section may collapse at the armhole. When using horsehair canvas or strong fusible interfacing this problem often is not visible immediately.

Often in combination with
- Stooped posture
- Rounded back
- S-shape posture

Rarely in combination with
- Fold at the neck
- Erect posture
- Asymmetrically square shoulders

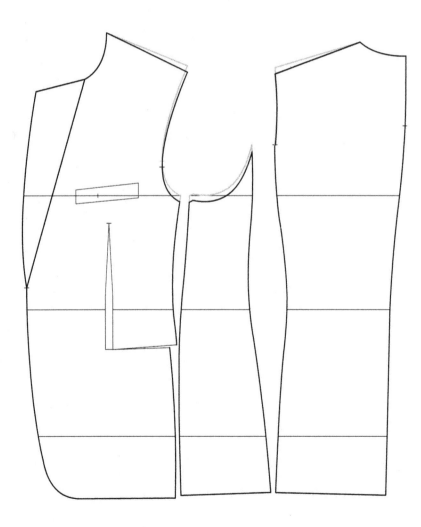

Changes to the pattern
- The shoulder seams at the armhole and the armhole are corrected downward, depending on the intensity of the sloping shoulder.
- Nothing changes at the neck.

For more information on shoulder height and padding thickness, see page 80.

To be considered during tailoring
- If the shoulders are asymmetrical, they can be compensated with different shoulder pads.
- Either a thicker pad is used for the sloping shoulder or a thinner pad for the normal shoulder.

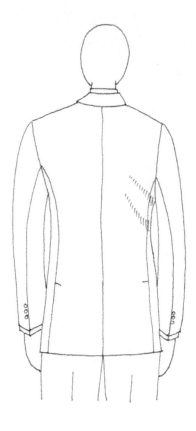

One-sided sloping shoulders
- One-sided sloping or low shoulders can occur in any body shape. This is often caused by one-sided strain or malpositions in the body.
- Look out for a one-sided strong hip!

Diagnosis
- Starting at the neck, diagonal folds are formed on the back toward the lower armhole area.

For more information on shoulder height and padding thickness, see page 80.

Changes to the pattern
The front
- At the side-part-seam, from the chest-line mark down approx. 5 cm.
- Draw a line to the pivot point *p1* and cut open.
- Rotate the front shoulder downwards by the required measurement using *p1*.
- The side-part-seam must be adjusted.

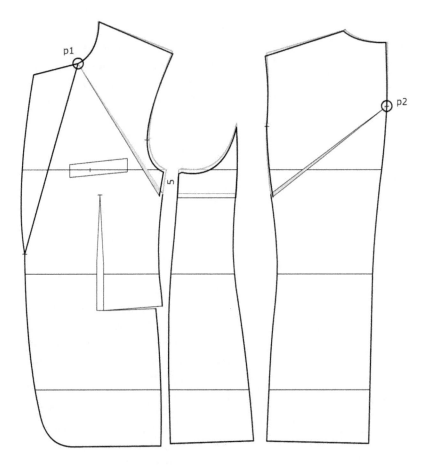

The back
- At the side-seam, from the chest-line mark down approx. 5 cm.
- Draw a line to the pivot point *p2* and cut open.
- Rotate the back shoulder downward by the required measurement using *p2* (like for the front).
- The side seam must be adjusted.

The side part
- At the side-part-seam and the side-seam, from the chest-line mark down approx. 5 cm.
- Drop down the side part by the required amount (as for the front piece).
- The side-part-seam and side-seam must be adjusted.

To be considered during tailoring
- If the shoulders are asymmetrical, they can be compensated with different shoulder pads. Either a thicker pad is used for the sloping shoulder or a thinner pad for the normal shoulder.

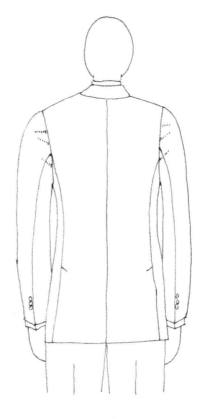

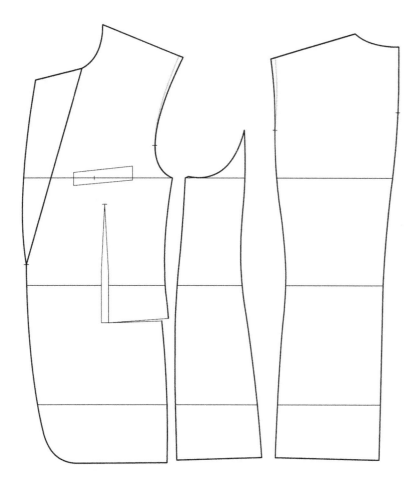

The shoulders are too narrow

- This does not apply if the jacket is generally too small, but only if the shoulders are too narrow.
- The upper arm pushes the sleeves outwards.
- The armhole seam at the shoulder should extend at least to the outer shoulder bone. If the upper arms are larger, it is possible to extend further.

Changes to the pattern

- At the front, the shoulder seam is extended by the desired measurement.
- The front armhole is balanced.
- For now, the armhole should not be cut out any further at the front (see page 108, front part pushes onto the arm); this can be inspected later.

- The shoulder seam on the back is extended by the same measurement.
- The back armhole is balanced.

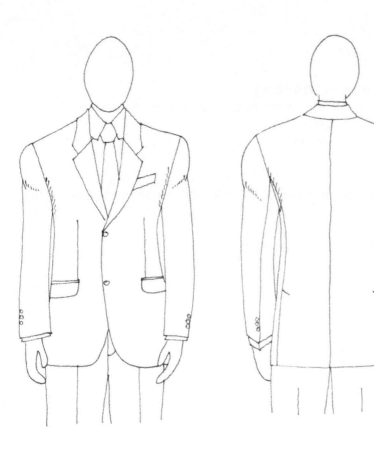

The shoulders are too wide

- This does not apply if the jacket is generally too large, but only if the shoulders are too wide.
- Attention, it is easy to overlook this error with thick shoulder pads. Here the shoulder does not clearly drop.
- The shoulder drops at the shoulder bone and hangs down (differentiation: sloping shoulders). The sleeve drops in the center of the sleeve head (not to be confused with: sleeve head is too high).

- The armhole seam at the shoulder should extend to the outer shoulder bone.
- In the case of more massive or muscular upper arms, the shoulder can also be slightly wider.

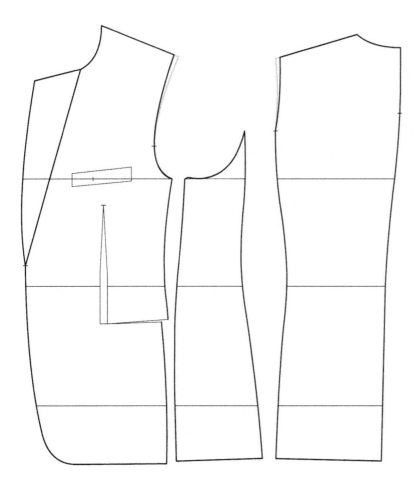

Changes to the pattern

- At the front, the shoulder seam is drawn narrower by the desired measurement.
- The front armhole is balanced.
- At the back, the shoulder seam is drawn narrower by the same amount.
- The back armhole is balanced.

Note

Most likely, the alteration for "the front part pushes onto arm" must also be included (see p. 108).

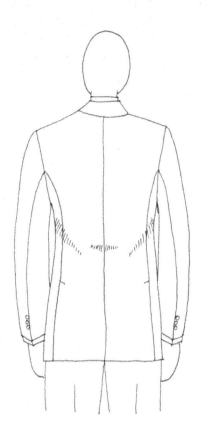

The back is too long

- Folds are formed on the back, running from the side seam towards the center back.
- The back is resting firmly on the seat and thus bulges in the waist area.

- When wearing a tailcoat or frock coat, the slit opens, and width is created on the tails.

Often in combination with
- Erect posture
- Square shoulders

Rarely in combination with
- Stooped posture
- Sloping shoulders

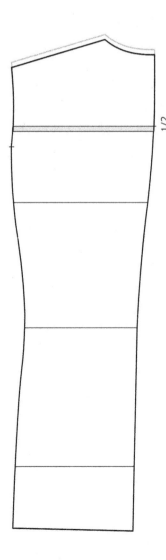

1/2

Changes to the pattern
- A line is drawn on the half depth-of-scye DOS parallel to the chest-line and cut open.
- The upper back is dropped down depending on the intensity (approx. 0.5 - 1 cm).

See also page 88 for more information on erect posture.

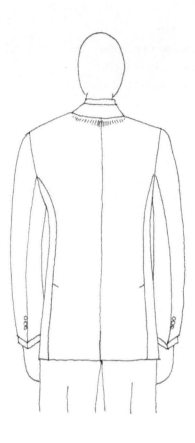

Fold at the neck

- In the back, a small horizontal fold is formed under the collar.
- The back neckline is not low enough; the collar was positioned too high.
- In contrast to "square shoulders" and "rounded shoulders", the fold at the neck is only noticeable on the back and does not extend to the shoulder.

Often in combination with

- Erect posture
- Square shoulders

Rarely in combination with

- Stooped posture
- Sloped shoulders

Changes to the pattern

- The neckline at the back and the inner shoulder at the neck are drawn lower by approx. 0.5 - 1 cm, depending on the intensity.

See page 80 for more information on shoulder height and shoulder pad thickness.

To be considered during tailoring

- A soft horsehair or wool interfacing is applied to the upper part of the back. This must be secured at the back seam and the shoulder seams. It prevents forming a fold at the neck if the collar has been placed only slightly too high up.

However, if the collar has been placed much too high, this action will not help at all.

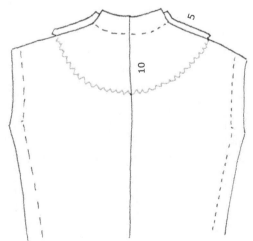

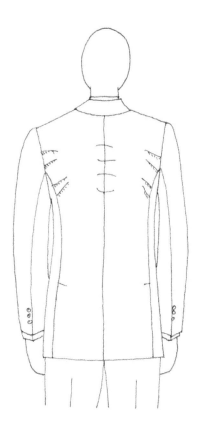

Strong shoulder blades

- The shoulder blades are pushed outward strongly.
- Between the shoulder blades, the back is tensed.
- Wrinkles form at the shoulder blades, pulling toward the armhole.

Often in combination with

- Stooped posture
- Rounded shoulders

Rarely in combination with

- Erect posture

Changes to the pattern

- First, lines are drawn as in the template below and then cut open.
- Part A is rotated slightly to the right using the pivot point *p1*.
- Part B is rotated slightly to the left using the pivot point *p2*.
- Part C is placed at Part B and rotated to the right using the pivot point *p3*.
- Part D is placed at the shoulder point of part C and rotated to the right using the pivot point *p4*.

To be considered during tailoring

- The back must be pressed properly.
- The shoulder blade area is stretched.
- The shoulder, the armhole, and the upper seam at the center back are kept short (see also p. 126).

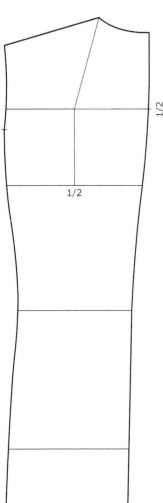

Preparing the pattern

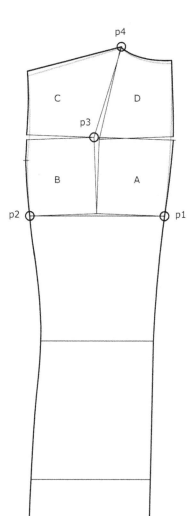

Opening the upper back

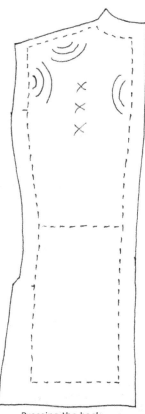

Pressing the back

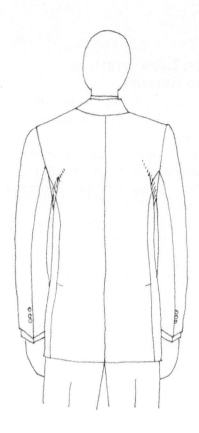

The back does not roll to the armhole

- The roll at the back (which serves as width for movement) collapses, the back does not fall nicely.

Often in combination with

- Sloping shoulders
- Erect posture

Rarely in combination with

- Stooped posture
- Square shoulders

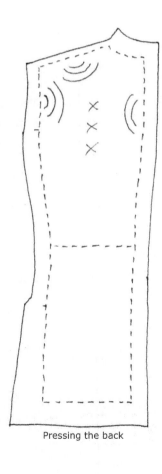

Pressing the back

Changes to the pattern

- The back shoulder seam is drawn lower by approx. 0.5 - 1 cm at the outside.

To be considered during tailoring

- The back must be pressed properly.
- The shoulder blade area is stretched.
- The shoulder, the armhole, and the upper seam at the center back are kept short (see also p. 126).

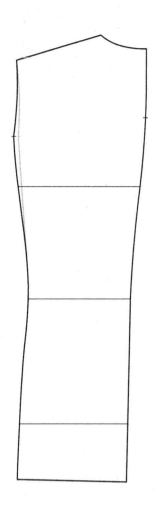

The back width is too narrow

- Horizontal tension folds form on the back across the shoulder blades.
- Not to be confused with strong shoulder blades (see p. 102).
- The material stretches across the back.
- The freedom of movement of the arms is restricted.

Changes to the pattern

- Above the waist-line the side seam is drawn slightly wider.
- The back armhole is adjusted accordingly.

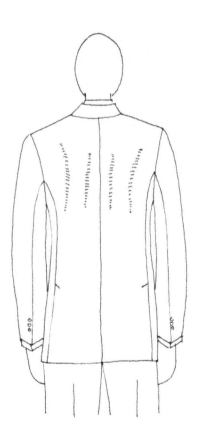
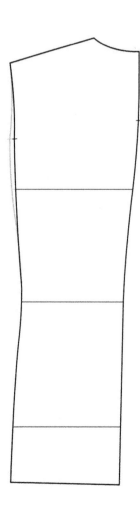

The back width is too wide

- Vertical folds form over the shoulder blades on the back.
- The material sits over the back very loosely.
- The width for the freedom of movement was measured very generously.

Changes to the pattern

- Above the waist-line, the side seam is drawn slightly narrower.
- The back armhole is adjusted accordingly.

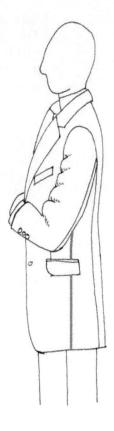

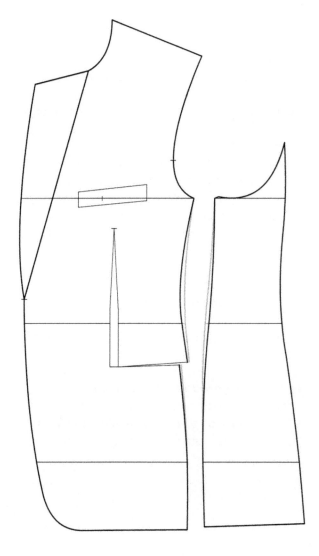

Shaping the jacket slim at the waist-line

A jacket can only get a slim waist-line at the side-part-seam.

The chest dart, as the name suggests, is used for the strength of the chest. At the side seam, the fit of the back and the width are changed.

Changes to the pattern
The front
- Approx. 3 cm above the waist-line, the side-part-seam is drawn narrower nicely.

The side
- Approx. 3 cm above the waist-line, the side-part-seam is drawn narrower nicely.

Less pronounced chest

- Ensure that it is actually a less pronounced chest and not a jacket that is generally too large.
- The customer appears rather slim and slender in a normal position.
- But even with a pointed belly, the chest area can sag.

Diagnosis

- The jacket collapses in the chest area.
- The fronts overlap in the chest area because the chest width is too wide or because too much chest width has been worked into the front.
- The front length can also be too long.

Often in combination with

- Rounded back
- S-shape posture

Rarely in combination with

- Erect posture
- Too much shoulder width

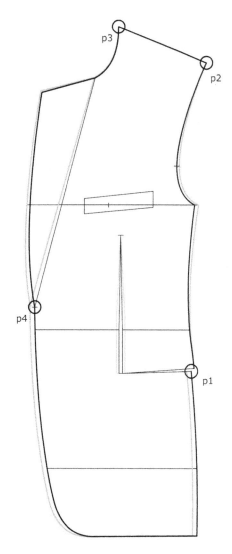

Changes to the pattern

- The chest area is drawn narrower at the chest-line.
- Using the pivot point *p1*, rotate the seam of the upper side-part-seam inwards by approx. 0.5 - 1 cm.
- Using the pivot point *p2*, the armhole is rotated in until it touches the new side-part-seam.
- Using the pivot point *p3*, rotate the front edge inwards by approx. 0.5 - 1 cm.
- The lower part of the edge is rotated straight again (parallel to the edge) using the pivot point *p4*.
- The dart is drawn narrower. Thus, the lower side-part-seam at the pocket must be adjusted again.
- The chest pocket may have to be drawn narrower.

To be considered during tailoring

- The chest area is pressed only slightly.
- The less pronounced chest is regarded in the canvas as well (smaller darts).

Strong chest

Not to be confused with the erect posture.
These customers are often singers, brass musicians, swimmers, or divers (large lung capacity).

Diagnosis
- If the jacket is closed, the lapel break sticks out in the chest area because the chest width is too narrow or because too little chest width has been worked into the front part.
- If the chest is very strong, the front-waist-length may also be too short.
- The lapel break was not kept short enough (see p. 126).

Often in combination with
- Erect posture
- Narrow width-of-scye

Rarely in combination with
- Rounded back
- Stooped posture
- Large shoulder width

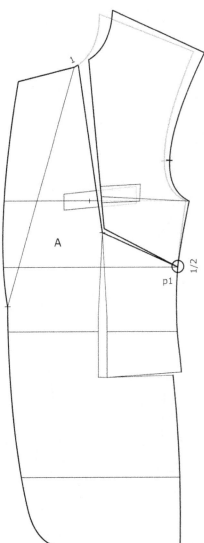

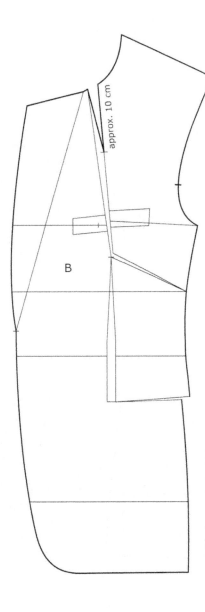

Changes to the pattern
A:
- Halve the distance between chest-line and waist-line.
- At the neckline at the lapel break mark to the right 1 cm.
- From here, draw a line to the dart
- From the dart, draw another line to the side piece seam.
- Now rotate open the front using the pivot point *p1* by approx. 1 - 1.5 cm.

B:
- The upper chest dart is approx. 10 cm long. It must be hidden under the lapel.

To be considered during tailoring
- The dart must disappear under the lapel.
- More chest is worked in during pressing (see p. 126).
- In addition, the lapel break is kept short.

The front pushes into the armhole

- The front pushes into the armhole and bulges at the front of the arm.
- The customer feels like the armhole pushes into the front of the arm.
- Not to be confused with the less pronounced chest (see p. 106).

Often in combination with
- Large shoulder width
- Less pronounced chest

Rarely in combination with
- Strong chest
- Erect posture

Changes to the pattern
- At the front, the armhole is cut out a little (approx. 0.5 cm) to the front and down.
- Due to the new depth-of-scye, the sleeve must be cut lower by approx. 0.4 cm (80% of the measurement by which the armhole was cut lower).

Note
It is important to ask the customer whether he feels pressure on the arm from the front or below because the armhole is too high (see p. 118).
Be careful when cutting out the armhole!

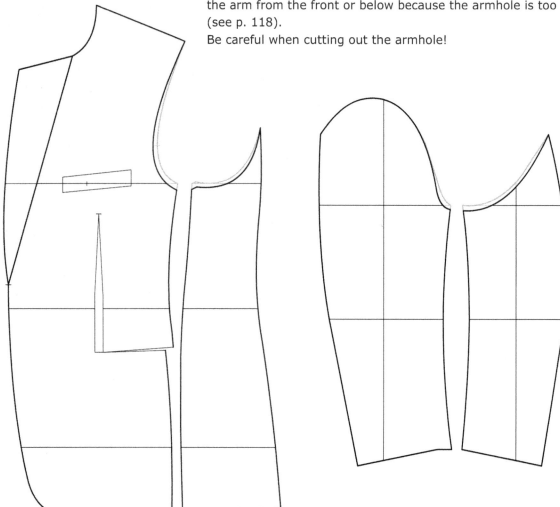

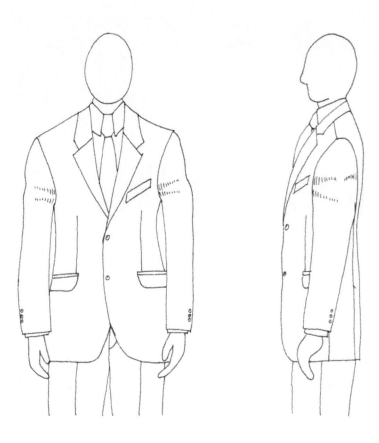

The armhole is cut out too far

- The sleeve pulls tight at the armhole
- The sleeve does not roll in the front (does not fall nicely) and is pulled out of balance.

Often in combination with
- Strong chest
- Erect posture

Rarely in combination with
- Less pronounced chest
- Stopped posture

Changes to the pattern
The front
- Here, an alteration is only possible at the first fitting, with a finished front edge, it is almost impossible.
- Because of this, enough seam allowance is considered during the cutting process.

The sleeve
- The sleeve is cut as for a pronounced belly. This is not perfect, but it takes the tension off the sleeve in the front.

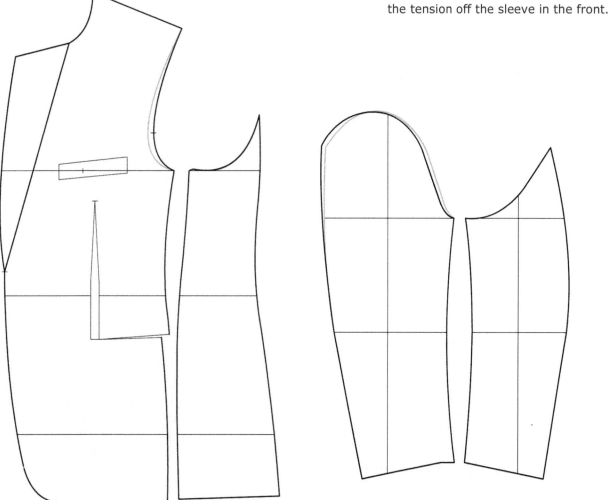

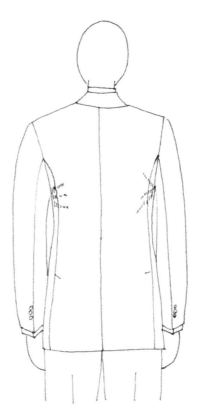
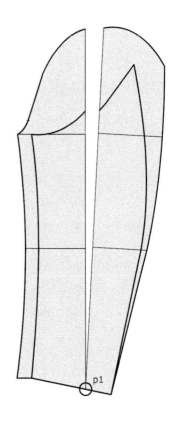

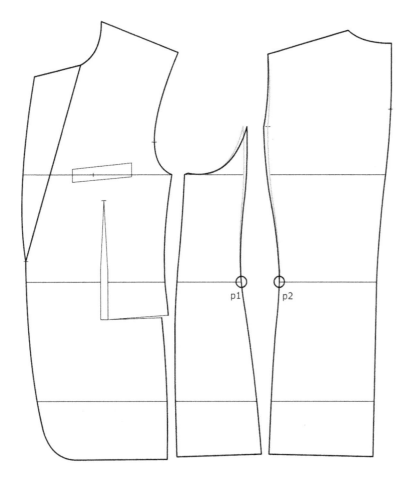

The width of scye is too narrow

- The width-of-scye is important for the range of movement at the chest and sleeves.
- The front armhole pushes against the customer's arm.
- This is common problem with athletic body shapes.

Changes to the pattern

The jacket
- The side part is rotated slightly to the right using the pivot point *p1*.
- The back is rotated slightly to the left using the pivot point *p2*.
- The armhole is adjusted
- This makes the chest looser, and the armhole no longer pushes against the front of the arm.

The sleeve
- The sleeve is now too small for the armhole and will be extended.
- The sleeve-center-line is cut open and the sleeve is extended using the pivot point *p1*. The affected seams must be adjusted.

Fitting errors at the jacket sleeve

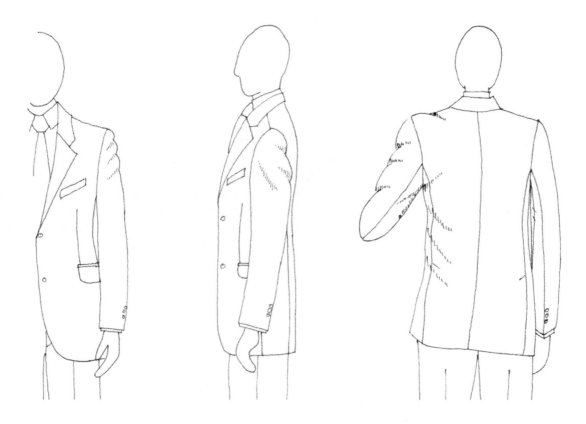

Sleeve is inserted
too high

Sleeve is inserted
too low

Wrong sleeve pitch

Since the sleeve pitch is different for each person, it makes no sense to mark the sleeve pitch in the pattern before the first fitting (see page 24)

Sleeve is inserted too high

Mark a few points (*a, b, c*) on the sleeve and on the jacket and move the points of the sleeve counterclockwise by the necessary amount.

Sleeve is inserted too low

Mark a few points (*a, b, c*) on the sleeve and on the jacket and move the points of the sleeve clockwise by the necessary amount.

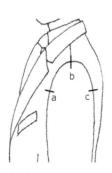  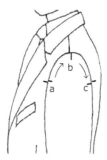

Mark sleeve points

Rotate sleeve counterclockwise

Rotate sleeve clockwise

Sleeve too long
at the back

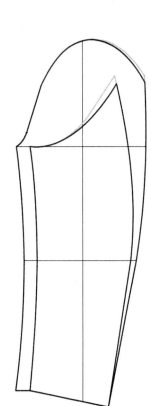

The sleeve is too long at the back

- Unlike the sleeve wich is inserted too low, only the back seam shows folds that do not extend to the front diagonally.

Changes to the pattern

- The back sleeve head is lowered by the necessary amount.
- The under sleeve is drawn lower by the same amount at the back seam.
- The sleeve may have to be slightly wider at the back seam.

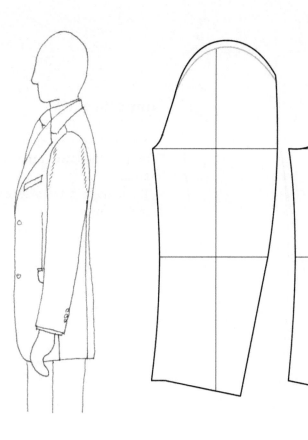

The sleeve head is too flat

- Vertical folds form on the sides of the sleeve head.
- When the sleeve head is lowered by pushing down the shoulder pad, the folds disappear, and the sleeve is smooth.

Changes to the pattern

The top sleeve:
- The sleeve head is too flat and has to be drawn higher by the necessary amount (e.g. 1 cm).
- The back seam is drawn higher by half the measurement (e.g. 0.5 cm).

The undersleeve:
- The back seam is drawn higher by half the measurement like the upper sleeve (e.g. 0.5 cm).
- If the sleeve has too much width for the armhole, this can be reduced at the back seam (see sleeve drawing on page 81).

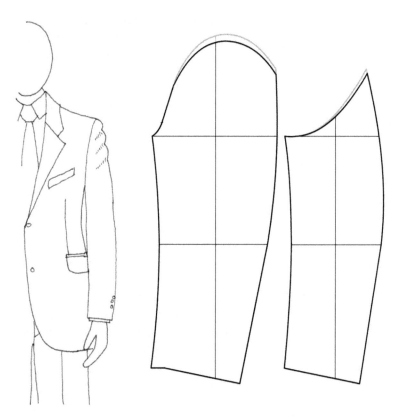

The sleeve head is too high

- Horizontal folds form on the sleeve head.
- If the sleeve head is pinned shorter at the top, the folds will dissolve and the sleeve will lie flat.

Changes to the pattern

The top sleeve:
- The sleeve head is too high and will be drawn lower by the necessary amount (e.g. 1 cm).
- The back seam is drawn lower by half the measurement (e.g. 0.5 cm).

The undersleeve:
- The back seam is drawn lower by half the measurement like the upper sleeve (e.g. 0.5 cm).
- If the sleeve has too little width for the armhole, this can be extended at the back seam (see sleeve drawing on page 81).

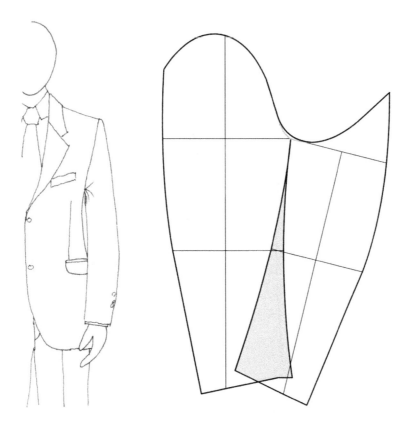

Imperfect fit
- On the top sleeve, diagonal wrinkles and "bags" form in the lower armhole area.
- It seems as if the sleeve is pulled inwards.

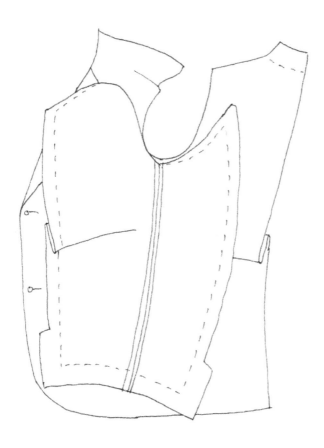

Changes to the pattern
- The course of the armhole and the front/side piece of the sleeve do not match up.
- The seam on the sleeve must be marked just as round and evenly as at the armhole.

To be considered during tailoring
- When basting or sewing the sleeve, make sure that the seam is even.
- The shape of the armhole and the sleeve must match up. Never pull the seam anywhere, just so that the sleeve supposedly fits into the armhole.
- With firm fabrics, a few millimeters too much or too little in the wrong places can prevent the sleeve from falling perfectly.

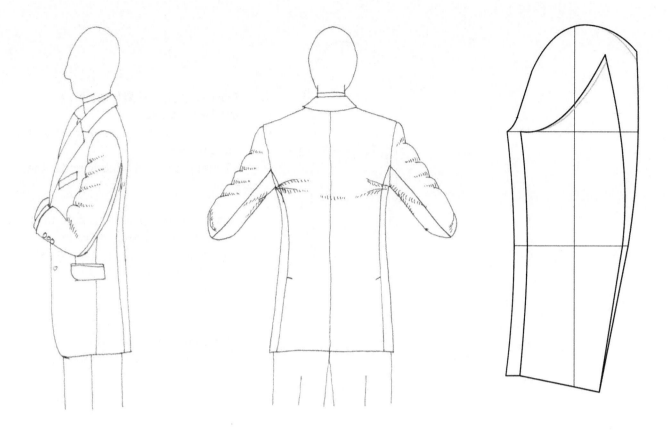

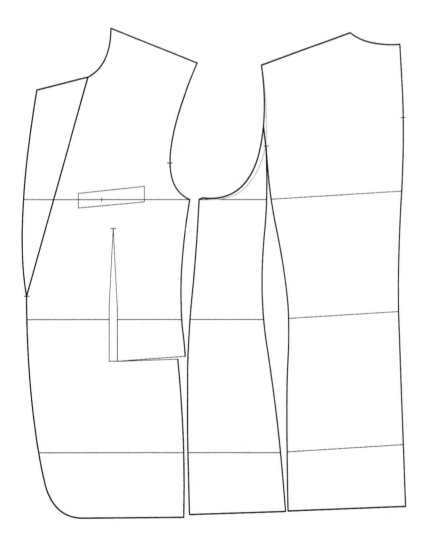

Tension at the back

- An uncomfortable sleeve can also be caused by the armhole being cut out too much in the back area.
- When the arm is moved forward, tension wrinkles form on the sleeve and back.
- Every arm movement feels constricting and uncomfortable.

Changes to the pattern

The sleeve

- The sleeve head needs more length at the back and is raised accordingly.

The side and back

- At the side and back part, the armhole shape is matched to the sleeve.
  Here, some width is required, the back armhole is cut out less.
- Place the side and back part against each other at the side seam so that the seam becomes even.

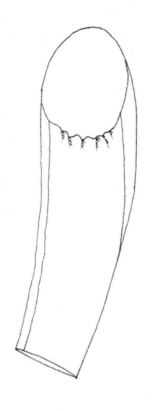

Too much width at the undersleeve

- Sack-like wrinkles are formed at the undersleeve.
- There is too much fabric under the arm.

This problem is actually a pure tailoring error. If the sleeve is too wide, sometimes an attempt is made to insert the excess width at the undersleeve.

Not to be confused with
- The sleeve head being too flat.

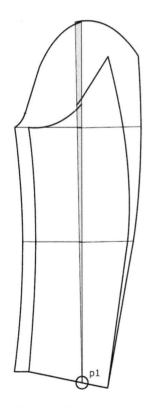

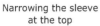
Narrowing the sleeve at the top

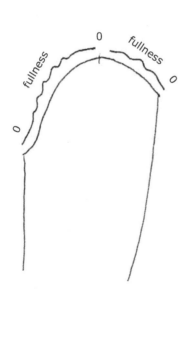

Changes to the pattern
- Instead of adding the excess width at the undersleeve, the sleeve should be tightened.
- The sleeve-center-line is cut open and the sleeve is narrowed using the pivot point *p1*.
- The affected seams must be adjusted.

You can also try to distribute the width more evenly. However, if a flat, narrow sleeve head is desired, you should make the sleeve narrower.

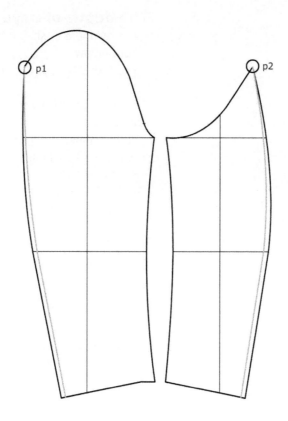

The sleeve hem is to narrow

- The sleeve gets caught on the shirt cuff or the watch and does not fall over it naturally.
- Maybe the forearm is too strong.
- When bending the elbow, the customer feels very constricted.

Changes to the pattern

- Using the pivot point $p1$, the top sleeve is rotated to the left.
- Using the pivot point $p2$, the undersleeve is rotated to the right.
- The sleeve length must be adjusted.

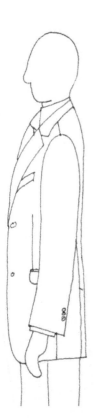

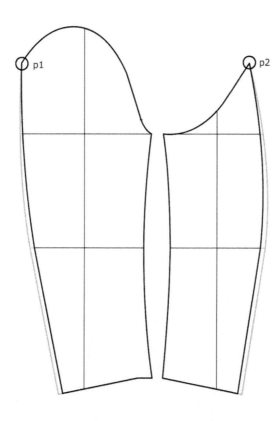

The sleeve hem is too wide

- The sleeve slackens around and does not fit the jacket proportionally.

Changes to the pattern

- Using the pivot point $p1$, the top sleeve is rotated to the right.
- Using the pivot point $p2$, the undersleeve is rotated to the left.
- The sleeve length must be adjusted.

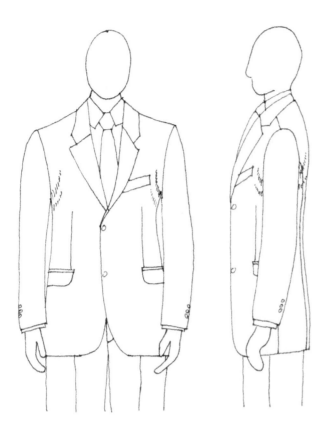

The depth-of-scye is too high

- The armhole pushes into the customer's armpit from below.
- The fabric bulges under the arm.

Changes to the pattern

The jacket:
- The armhole is cut out lower according to the customer's wishes.

  Benchmarks:
  - slight: 0.5 cm
  - medium: 1 cm
  - strong: 1.5 cm

The sleeve:
- The sleeve must be cut out lower because of the new depth-of-scye (approx. 80% of the measurement by which the armhole was cut out).
- This makes the sleeve head higher, and the sleeve fits into the armhole again.

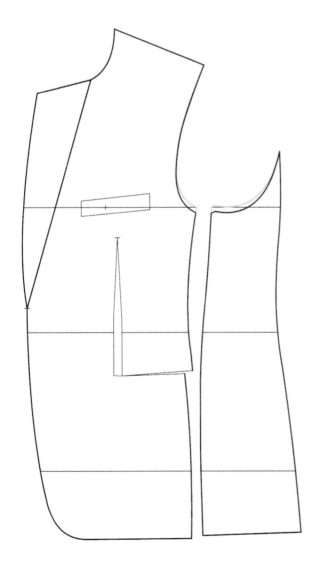

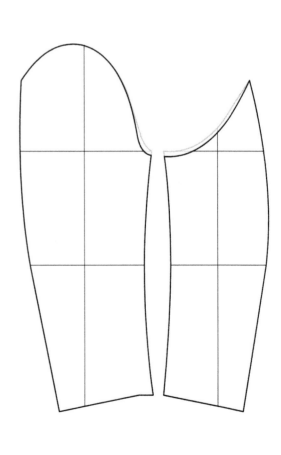

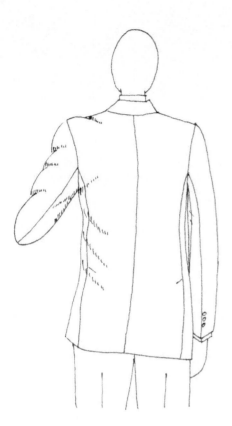

The depth-of-scye is too low

- The armhole restricts the customer's freedom of movement.
- The jacket moves along with every movement.
- When lifting the arm, the shoulder comes up to the ears.
- Under the arm, the "bat-sleeve-effect" is created.

Changes to the pattern

The jacket:
- If there are seam allowances, the depth-of-scye is marked
  higher according to the customer's wishes.
  Benchmarks:
  - slight: 0.5 cm
  - medium: 1 cm
  - strong: 1.5 cm

The sleeve, practical alteration:
- At the top sleeve, the sleeve head is drawn flatter (about
  80% of the measure by which the depth-of-scye was lowered).
  This makes the sleeve head smaller, and the sleeve fits into
  the armhole again.
- The sleeve length must be adjusted.

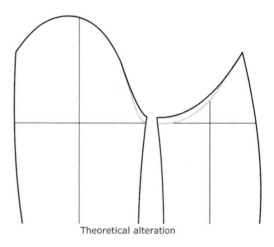

Theoretical alteration

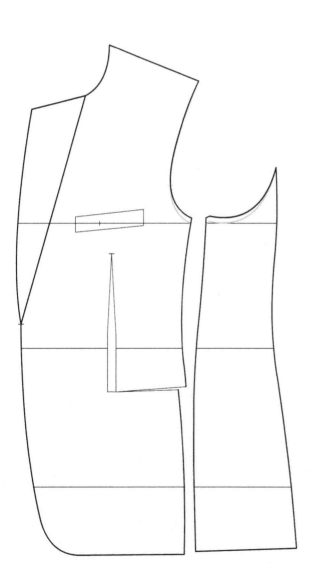

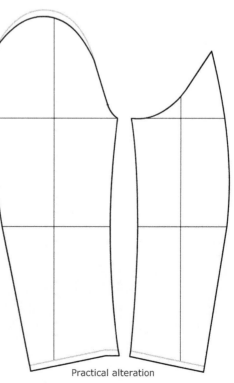

Practical alteration

Fitting errors at the neckline
and jacket collar

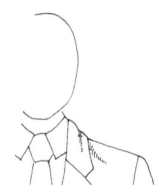

The neckline is too narrow
- The collar is pushed outwards by the neck.
- This causes wrinkles under the collar and on the top collar.

Often in combination with
- Strong chest (e.g. with bodybuilders or singers).

Changes to the pattern
The front
- The shoulder seam is marked narrower at the neckline.
- The front neckline has to be adjusted.

The back
- The shoulder seam is marked narrower at the neckline.
- The back neckline has to be adjusted.

Alternatively:
- The center back *CB* is slightly widened.

The neckline is too wide

- There is a gap at the side between the neck and the collar. Either the neck is very slender, or the neckline was generally drawn too wide when drawing the pattern.

Often in combination with

- Rounded back
- Stooped posture
- S-shape posture
- Square shoulders

Changes to the pattern

The front
- The shoulder seam is extended toward the neck.
- The front neckline is adjusted.

The back
- The shoulder seam is extended toward the neck.
- The back neckline is adjusted.

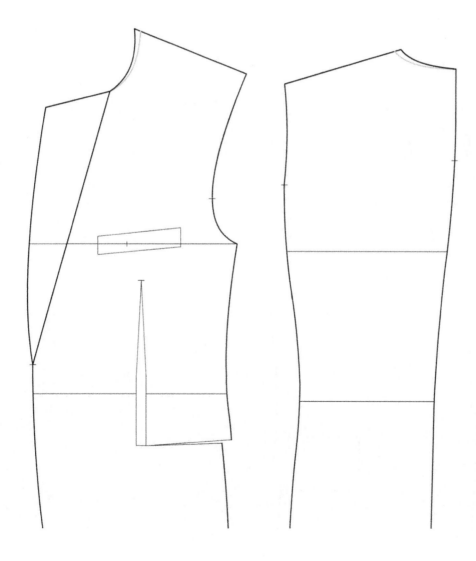

The collar is too low

- The collar may appear too low on a very long neck or a shirt with a high collar.
- A well-fitting shirt is important for the fitting.
- The shirt collar should stick out by approx. 1 - 1.5 cm from the jacket collar.

Diagnosis

- The upper edge of the jacket's top collar is very low.
- The shirt collar sticks out too much.

Often in combination with

- Erect posture
- Sloped shoulders

Changes to the pattern

- The lapel break and the lapel are moved forward using the pivot point *p1*.
- At the under collar, the collar stay at the undercollar must be drawn higher by the same amount.

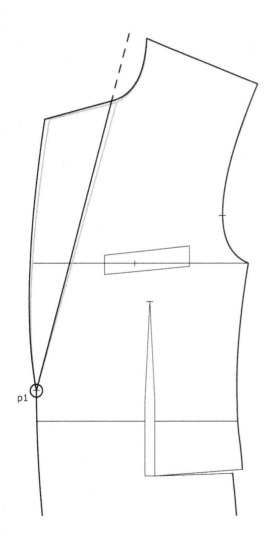

The collar is too short

- Tension wrinkles form at the top collar in the direction to the gorge seam.
- The undercollar was attached to the lapel in the front area with too much tension.

Changes to the pattern

- A new undercollar must be made.
- The collar must be lengthened a little towards the front.

To be considered during tailoring

Undercollar 1 (Picture down left)
- The undercollar is attached from the center back, across the shoulder seam to the front, evenly and without tension.

Undercollar 2 (Picture down right)
- The lapel is now tightened slightly (a few millimeters) at the gorge seam and attached to the undercollar.

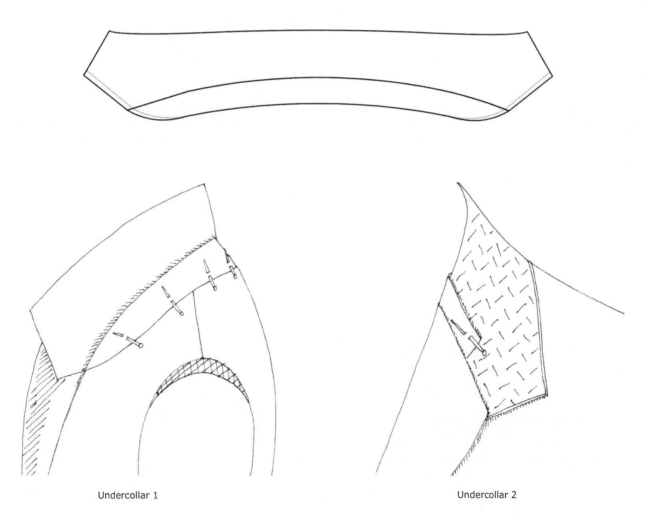

Undercollar 1   Undercollar 2

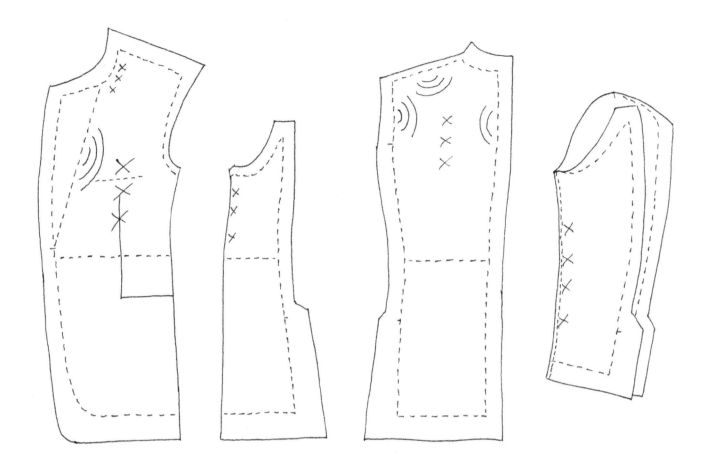

Pressing the jacket
The front
Both front pieces should be placed with the right sides facing each other and ironed into shape evenly.

- The lapel break is kept short.
- The armhole is kept short for strong chests.
- The upper part at the neckline is slightly stretched for the shoulder.
- The chest area is slightly stretched.

The side
Both side pieces should be placed with the right sides facing each other and ironed into shape evenly.

- The side-part-seam is slightly stretched.

The back
Both back pieces should be placed with the right sides facing each other and ironed into shape evenly.

- The shoulder blade area is stretched.
- The shoulder and the armhole are kept short.
- The upper center back seam is slightly kept short.

The sleeve
The sleeve is pressed after the top- and undersleeves are sewn together.

- The front sleeve seam is slightly stretched.
- Only now, the front sleeve seam is ironed flat; the fabric pattern of the undersleeve should lay perfectly straight during the pressing process.

Note
- In case of stripes or checks, the fabric pattern must be even and not warped.
- Throughout the entire process, care should be taken to ensure that the armhole and the lapel break do not stretch again.

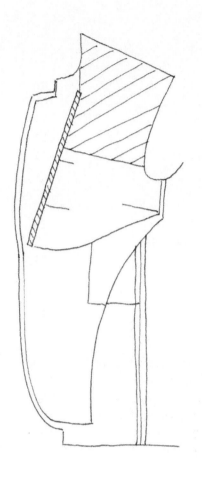

Stabilizing the lapel break

To prevent the lapel break from expanding, it is held in place using a linen or lining tape.

- Approx. 1 cm behind the lapel break line, a linen tape is pinned on and then sewn with a blind- or slip-stitch.
- Depending on the strength of the chest of the wearer, it should be kept short to a greater or lesser extent.
- Usually, it is sufficient to fix the tape approx. 1 cm shorter.
- Of course, a fusible tape can also be used.

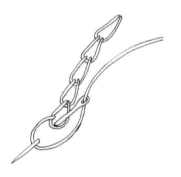

Stabilizing the armhole

- The armhole is kept short with a chain stitch.

Preparing the back

- A soft horsehair or wool canvas is applied inside to the upper part of the back. This must be secured at the center back seam and at the shoulder seams. It prevents the creation of a fold at the neck.

- Throughout the entire tailoring process, care should be taken to ensure that the armhole and shoulder seam at the back does not stretch again.

Index

A

Attaching the undercollar	125

B

Back pants length	12
Back width	11
Body height	12
Bowlegs	41

C

Chest	10
Chest width	10
Circumference of scye	17
Collar is too low	124
Collar is too short	125

D

Depth of breast	11
Depth of scye	11
Depth of stomach	13

E

Ease at the back	50
Erect posture	20
Erect posture, sleeve	78
Extending the crotch	48
Extending the hem girth	56
Extending the thigh girth	54
Extending the waistband	42

F

Fit of the Jacket	29
Fit of the vest	30
Fit of the pants	31
Fit of the shirt	32
Fitting	24
Fitting errors at the jacket	77
Fitting errors at the jacket sleeve	111
Fitting errors at the neckline	121
Fitting errors at the pants	33
Fitting errors at the vest	59
Fitting, adjusting the front	26
Fitting, aligning the back	25
Fitting, attaching the collar	27
Fitting, attaching the shoulder	26
Fitting, balance control	27
Fitting, collar position	28
Fitting, pinning the shoulder	27
Fitting, securing the back	25
Fitting, shoulder width	28
Fitting, smoothing out the back	24

F

Flat seat	46
Fold at the neck	101
Front pants length	12
Front waist length	11
Full shoulder width	11

H

Height	12
Hip	10
Hip stronger on one side	39
Increasing the rise	51

I

Inside leg	12

J

Jacket, armhole is cut out too far	109
Jacket, back does not roll	103
Jacket, back too long	100
Jacket, back width too narrow	104
Jacket, back width too wide	104
Jacket, erect posture	88
Jacket, fold at the neck	101
Jacket, front pushes into the armhole	108
Jacket, less pronounced chest	106
Jacket, one-sided sloping shoulder	97
Jacket, narrow shoulders	98
Jacket, pressing	126
Jacket, rounded back	84
Jacket, rounded shoulders	94
Jacket, S-shape posture	86
Jacket, seat too tight	92
Jacket, seat too wide	93
Jacket, shaping the jacket	105
Jacket, sloping shoulders	96
Jacket, square shoulders	95
Jacket, stooped posture	82
Jacket, strong chest	107
Jacket, strong shoulder blades	102
Jacket, too tight	90
Jacket, too loose	91
Jacket, wide shoulders	99
Jacket, width of scye is too narrow	110

K

Knock knees	40

L

Less pronounced hip curve	45
Lowering the rise	51
Lowering the waistband	37

M

Measurement sheet   134

N

Nape to front waist   11
Nape to knee   12
Nape to waist-length   11
Neck   10
Neckline is too narrow   122
Neckline is too wide   123
Neckline, collar is too low   124
Neckline, collar is too short   125
Normal posture   20

O

Outside leg   12

P

"Package" not considered   52
"Package" considered wrongly   52
Pants, bow legs   41
Pants, pleat opens up   53
Pants, ease at the back   50
Pants, extending the crotch   48
Pants, extending the hem girth   56
Pants, extending the thigh girth   54
Pants, extending the waistband   42
Pants, flat seat   46
Pants, hip stronger on one side   39
Pants, increasing the rise   51
Pants, ironing into shape   58
Pants, knock knees   40
Pants, less pronounced hip curve   45
Pants, lowering the rise   51
Pants, lowering the side seam   36
Pants, package not considered   52
Pants, package considered wrongly   52
Pants, pelvis tilted backward   35
Pants, pelvis tilted forward   34
Pants, pelvis tilted sideways   38
Pants, pressing the pants properly   58
Pants, raising the side seam   37
Pants, reducing the crotch   49
Pants, reducing the hem girth   57
Pants, reducing the waistband   43
Pants, reducing the thigh girth   55
Pants, strong seat   47
Pants, stronger hip curve   44
Pants, too much room at the back   50
Pants, too tight at the calf   53
Pattern alteration sheet   133
Pelvis tilted backward   35
Pelvis tilted forward   34
Pelvis tilted sideways   38

P

Posture, erect   20
Posture, normal   20
Posture, S-shape   20
Posture, stooped   20
Posture, pronounced belly   20
Posture, strong chest   20
Posture, rounded back   20
Preparing the back   127
Pressing the jacket   126
Pressing the pants properly   58
Pressing the sleeve   126
Pressing the vest   76
Pronounced belly   20

R

Rounded back   20
Raising the waistband   36
Reducing the crotch   49
Reducing the hem girth   57
Reducing the waistband   43
Reducing the thigh girth   55
Rounded shoulders, jacket   94

S

Shoulder angle   13
Shoulder width   10
Shoulderpads   80
Shoulders, normal   80
Shoulders, retracted   79
Shoulders, rounded   79
S-shape posture   20
Sleeve, angled   81
Sleeve, before cutting   78
Sleeve, depth of scye too high   118
Sleeve, depth of scye too low   119
Sleeve, erect posture   78
Sleeve head too high   113
Sleeve head too low   113
Sleeve, hem too narrow   117
Sleeve, hem too wide   117
Sleeve, imperfect fit   114
Sleeve, inserted too high   112
Sleeve, inserted too low   112
Sleeve length   11
Sleeve pitch   112
Sleeve pitch   24
Sleeve, pressing   126
Sleeve, retracted shoulders   79
Sleeve, rounded shoulders   79
Sleeve, stooped posture   78
Sleeve, strong upper arm   81
Sleeve, tension at the back   115
Sleeve, tightening   81

S

Sleeve, too long at the back	112
Sleeve, widening	81
Sleeve, width at the under sleeve	116
Sleeve, wrong sleeve pitch	112
Sloping shoulders, jacket	96
Square shoulders, jacket	95
Stabilizing the armhole	127
Stabilizing the lapel break	127
Stooped posture	20
Stooped posture, sleeve	78
Strong chest	20
Strong seat	47
Stronger hip curve	44

T

Taking measurements	9
Thigh	13
Too much room at the back	50
Too tight at the calf	53

U

Under-belly waistband	13
Undercollar	125
Upper arm	10

V

Vest, armhole is too high	74
Vest, armhole is too low	74
Vest, armhole sticks out	69
Vest, back is too long	75
Vest, back is too short	75
Vest, edges overlap too much	67
Vest, erect posture	63
Vest, front armhole is bulging	71
Vest, front armhole is cut out too far	71
Vest, front is too short	68
Vest, front opening sticks out	69
Vest, ironing into shape	76
Vest, lower front edge sticks out	66
Vest, neckline too close	70
Vest, pressing properly	76
Vest, stabilizing the opening	76
Vest, rounded back	61
Vest, S-shape posture	62
Vest, shoulders are too narrow	73
Vest, shoulders are too wide	73
Vest, sloping shoulders	72
Vest, square shoulders	72
Vest, stooped posture	60
Vest, strong chest	68
Vest, too tight	64
Vest, too loose	65

W

Waist-length	11
Waistband	10
Waistline	10
Width of cuffs	13
Width of length (pants)	13

Abbreviations

B

BPL	Back pants length
BRW	Breast width
BSA	Back shoulder angle
BW	Back-width

C

CAL	Calf
CB	Center back
CF	Center front
CHE	Chest
COS	Circumference of scye
CVP	Cervical vertebra point

D

DOB	Depth of breast
DOS	Depth of scye

F

FPL	Front pants length
FSA	Front shoulder angle
FSH	Front shoulder
FUSH	Full shoulder
FWL	Front waist length

H

HEI	Height
HIP	Hip

I

INL	Inside leg

L

LG	Length

N

NE	Neck
NTK	Nape to knee

O

OUTL	Outside leg

P

P	Pivot point

S

SA	Shoulder angle
SH	Shoulder width
SL	Sleeve length
SLH	Sleeve head
SLHW	Sleeve hem width

U

UBWB	Underbelly waistband

W

WAI	Waist
WB	Waistband
WL	Waist-length
WOC	Width of cuff
WOL	Width of leg
WOS	Width of scye
WR	Wrist

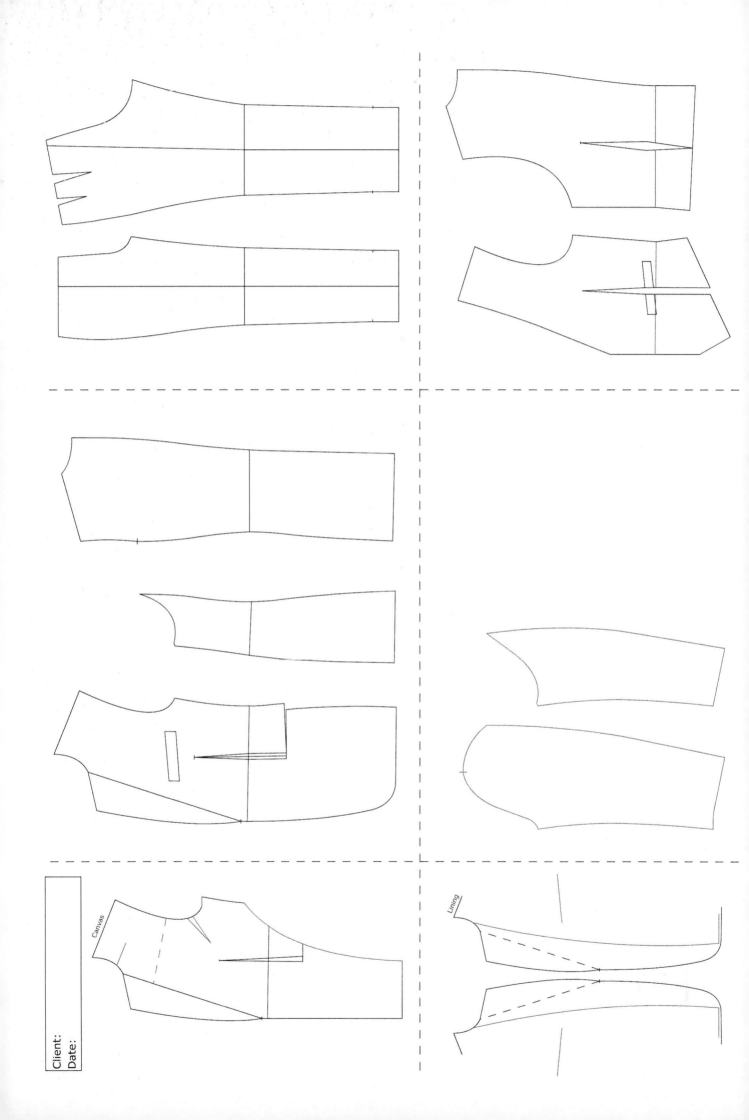

Client:
Date:

Canvas

Lining

Measurement sheet for men

Name:		Billing address:
Phone:		

Date:

HEI	Body height			
NE	Neck			
CHE	Chest			
WAI	Waist			
WB	Waistband			
UBWB	Under belly waistband			
HIP	Hips			
FUSH	Full shoulder			
SH R/L	Shoulder R/L			
SA R/L	Shoulderangle R/L			
BW	Back width			
DOS	Depth of scye			
WL	Waist length			
LG	Length			
NTK	Nape to knee			
CLG	Coat length			
DOB	Depth of breast			
FWL	Front waist length			
DST	Depth of belly			
CW	Chest width			
SL	Sleeve length R/L			
UPA	Upper arm			
FO	Forearm			
WR	Wrist			
OUTL	Outside leg			
FPL	Front pants length			
BPL	Back pants length			
INL	Inside leg			
TH	Thigh			
KN	Knee band			
CAL	Calf			
WOL	Width of length			

Order

Fabric:	Lining:

Extras

Posture

stooped ☐
normal ☐
erect ☐
rounded back ☐
hollow back ☐
belly ☐

Shoulder

rounded ☐   retracted ☐
square ☐ normal ☐ slope ☐

Chest

strong ☐   flat ☐

Hips

strong ☐   flat ☐

Seat

strong ☐   flat ☐

Jacket

Single breasted ☐   Double breasted ☐   Chest pocket ☐
Buttons at CF _____   Ticket pocket ☐
Lapel, notched ☐   peaked ☐   Buttons at sleeve ____
Vent,   side ☐   back ☐   none ☐
Jetted pockets, straight ☐   slanted ☐

Lining pockets

Pants

Zip ☐   Buttons ☐   Crease ☐
Front pockets, slanted ☐   inseam ☐   jetted ☐
Seat pockets R ☐   L ☐   Waistband extension ☐
Turn-up ☐   Buckle loop CF ☐
Belt loops ☐   Buckle straps ☐

Vest

Single breasted ☐   Double breasted ☐
Buttons at CF _____
Pockets _____   welted ☐   jetted ☐
Lapel, notched ☐   peaked ☐   none ☐
Vent, side ☐   back ☐   none ☐

Consent to data storage

I hereby consent to the analog and digital storage of the above data and the pattern.
The data will not be shared with third parties.

_____

Date

_____

Signature

MODERN MEN'S TAILORING
A BASIC GUIDE TO PATTERN DRAFTING

Sven Jungclaus   Michael Ross

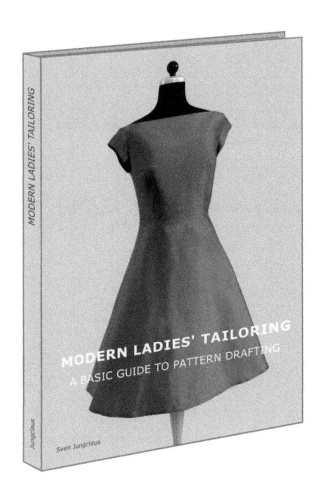

MODERN LADIES' TAILORING
A BASIC GUIDE TO PATTERN DRAFTING

Sven Jungclaus

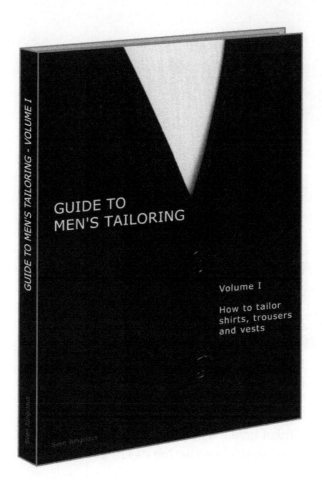

You will find information about the books and more on our website
www.becomeatailor.com

Sven Jungclaus

completed his training as a bespoke ladies' and men's tailor in the 1990s with *Heinz-Josef Radermacher* in Dusseldorf. At that time, he already worked for musical productions like *Grease* and *Forever Plaid* in Dusseldorf as well as *The Beauty and the Beast* and *The Fearless Vampire Killers* in Stuttgart.

After eight years at the *Bavarian State Opera* in Munich as a master tailor and head of men's costume, he has deepened his expertise at the *Royal Shakespeare Company* in Stratford upon Avon, the *Deutsche Oper am Rhein* in Dusseldorf, and the *Salzburg Festival*.

Since 2013, he has been producing bespoke clothing for men and women in his tailor shop in Salzburg. In addition, the versatile tailor works again and again for the costume workshop *Das Gewand* in Dusseldorf and is requested for operas or musical productions - e.g., the *Metropolitan Opera* in New York, the *Nasjonale Opera* in Bergen, the *Theater Basel*, the Musical *Chicago* in Stuttgart and Berlin, *Het Muziektheater* in Amsterdam, the *Salzburg Festival* or the *Theater of Nations in Moscow*.

Another project of Sven Jungclaus is *Become-a-tailor*, an internet presence with professional tips on workmanship, patterns, and instructions as well as other know-how for many costume epochs.

www.becomeatailor.com

CPSIA information can be obtained
at www.ICGtesting.com
Printed in the USA
BVHW011007030122
625349BV00016B/456